THROUGH A DAUGHTER'S EYES

Forty-Nine Years as Her Child;
Forty-Nine Days as Her Caregiver.

Natalie Manns

Edited by Denise Stern, Gemini Writing Services

ISBN: 1499630751
ISBN 13: 9781499630756

Much Love

To Opal Jean,
who would hate all of this attention and is most likely trying
to find a way to get the last word;

To my Bunny, Gregor,
who somehow manages to "get" me and loves me regardless;

To Tonya,
who knows all my childhood secrets and continues to be my
best friend;

And to my Siblings and Relatives,
who are missing Mom's homemade rolls as much as the
woman who made them.

INTRODUCTION

In the 40-some years that I knew my mother, there was not one day I can recall where she had ever been ill. She was always the picture of health as she enjoyed an active life filled with swimming, bowling, bingo, and Clint Eastwood movies. She never let fear run her life and she never, ever, followed the crowd. When it came to life, religion and politics, my mother danced to the beat of her own drum.

Opal Jean was a force to be dealt with and no one, let alone a doctor, could tell her what to do. She was outspoken, opinionated, and loved a challenge. Her life was a mix of faith, humor, strength and poignancy.

This is my personal account of all the stories, tales and wisdom that was my mother, Opal Jean Edmond. Many of the events noted are accounts that came directly from her, which I have accumulated over the course of our lives together. Many are my own observations, experiences, and subsequent final moments I shared with her before she died on March 9, 2005.

To all of her friends and family members who read this and for those who never knew her, I write this out of the love I have for my mother. And while certain accounts may sound unpleasant or critical of her, in no way does it mean I harbor any disrespect or anger toward such a great and loving woman.

As with all relationships, there is the good as well as the challenging, mother-daughter drama. And if you knew my mother, you knew she was never one to hold back on what she considered her "truth"; so neither shall I.

~Natalie ~

1

OPAL JEAN - THE EARLY YEARS

Ever since I was a kid growing up with Mom and my brother, Gordon, in Fort Wayne, Indiana, I knew that she could stand toe-to-toe with the best of them. Anyone who ever knew Opal Jean knew you were in for a battle if you ever crossed her. Some thought because she was raised in the small town of Ardmore, Oklahoma, she was just a "hick" who could easily be taken advantage of. This was certainly far from the truth.

The oldest of three girls and one boy, Opal Jean Wesley lived a modest life: first in the remote town of Ardmore and then later in Oklahoma City. Her father, a sharecropper, passed away when she was a teenager. Her mother was a homemaker who made and sold beautiful handmade quilts and did laundry for people.

Opal Jean attended school in Ardmore and excelled in her studies. Loving music and singing, my mother used to perform in choirs and was often asked to sing the National Anthem at school events.

When she graduated from high school, Opal Jean felt ready to venture out into the world. She told her mother she wanted to go "up north," and at the age of eighteen, left home to pursue a singing career in New York City. This adventure took her first to St. Louis, Missouri, where she visited with relatives, and then to Fort Wayne, Indiana, visiting more relatives and taking on odd jobs as she made her way to New York.

In retrospect, she did admit to being "green" when she left home at such a young age. Here she was, this naïve, eighteen-year-old "colored" girl traipsing around the country *alone*. Still, Mom always contended, *"God looks out for babies and fools,"* and she believed that angels must have been watching over her. She was always fortunate enough to run into decent people who looked out for her so no one could take advantage of her. That belief served as the foundation that would shape her world for the rest of her life. To support herself as she traveled, my mother found work as a secretary; she never took a handout from anyone.

It was inevitable that my mother would fall in love and marry, but she had not planned on becoming a wife anytime soon. While visiting in Fort Wayne, my mother met and courted the man who would eventually sweep her off her feet and become my father. Cletus, "Greek", Edmonds was known by everyone as one of the local "players".

He was called Greek because he would *speak-so-quickly-that-folks-had-a-hard-time-understanding-what-he-said*, which made people think he was speaking in Greek. My father was notorious for doting on young, virginal women and my mother was ripe for the picking.

Handsome, suave, and too cool for words, Greek and my mother did what came naturally and were married a few years later... so much for New York.

Early on, my mother had an aversion to doctors when it came to her health, and anyone else's. When it came to sex, she had been given very little, if any, sex education. Therefore, when she thought she might be pregnant with my brother, she didn't know what to do. She disclosed her suspicions to her friends, who insisted she see a doctor. She finally did go, albeit begrudgingly.

The doctor confirmed that she was pregnant, but he was also alarmed. During his examination, he discovered that my mother had an ectopic pregnancy, carrying my brother in her fallopian tube. The doctor told my mother that she could not carry the child to term because neither she nor the child would survive. He strongly advised her to be admitted into the hospital for surgery, but my mother would not hear of it. Mom said she left his office and never went back to him, or any doctor, throughout the remainder of her pregnancy. Her attitude was, *"What do doctors know about my body?"* When she shared this story with me, all I could think was, *"God does look out for babies and fools..."*

When my mother was seven months along with my brother, she went into labor, bleeding and suffering from diarrhea. My father rushed her to the hospital, where her situation was soon deemed critical. When the doctor met with my father, he was told that things did not look good for either my mother or the baby.

The doctor then asked my father to make the choice to save either his wife or the baby if matters grew worse. Well, little did the doctor know that this was the *wrong* thing to ask of my father. All hell broke loose as my father went berserk. He grabbed the doctor by the collar and pushed him against the wall.

Mom said my father recalled asking himself, *"What am I going to do with a baby?"* and, after calming down, told the doctor to do what he could to save his wife.

After what seemed like forever, and through the grace of God, they were able to save both my mother and my *nine-pound* "preemie" brother, Gordon Robert. Other than being here a bit early, Gordon was a healthy baby. The doctor told my mother she was quite fortunate, although she did end up losing one of her fallopian tubes. He also told my mother that she would never be able to have any more children, nor should she try to, as it would kill her.

Of course, Opal Jean was not hearing that. *"What do doctors know about my body?"*

Because she put her faith in God and not the doctors, my mother continued to love my father and they let nature run its course. Four years later, a little girl with big brown eyes, who they named Natalie Renee, was born. No problems, no complications, and no fights with doctors.

Of course, the latter was thwarted because my father had already been banned from coming back to the hospital after the ruckus he caused during my brother's birth. Could you blame him?

Life continued along. I watched my mother's strength grow each year, even as my parent's marriage grew strained. Don't get me wrong, my mother loved my father until the day she died, but now, with the benefit of hindsight, the things he would ask her to do just did not make sense to me. Imagine this: if your siblings (from his previous marriage), aunts, and uncles all share the name EDMONDS, why in the hell would you want to change your name to EDMOND?

Well, that's exactly what Dad told Mom he wanted to do early in their relationship before my brother was born. Mom went along with this, much to the scrutiny of Dad's side of the family. As a kid, I never understood why my relatives would sit around and argue with Dad about their name. I did not realize the truth until I was a teenager, looking at a copy of my birth certificate, and saw no "S" at the end of my name. My older siblings, Cletus Jr. and Linda, from our father's first marriage, had the "S"; my cousins and uncles had the "S". Then here we come along, my father, mother, brother and I, with no "S".

Why in the world did my mother agree to such nonsense? It was an awkward and embarrassing thing to try and explain to folks. However, as a kid, what could I do? I never realized, until I was an adult, how much that omission of a single letter would cause such a rift between my relatives and me.

Who knew this was part of my father's then unknown nor spoken of, bout with schizophrenia. Odd requests like this were just the tip of the iceberg. Dad would experience bizarre moments of anger toward us kids and provoke fights with his co-workers at this factory job.

I even remember one long, quiet drive we took to Richmond, Indiana to drop him off at a place I later realized was the state's mental health hospital. He had been ordered by his job to go there for treatment due to his outbursts at work.

No one spoke about such things back then and not much was done for him except for the self-medicating he did with alcohol before and after his release. Needless to say, Mom never believed that Dad was mentally ill despite his eventual diagnosis later in life.

Whatever his problem was, my mother grew weary of his behavior. Once, his anger caused him to give my brother a black eye with the belt buckle during a butt whoopin'. Other kids got "spankings"; my brother and I got butt *whoopin's*. I received my share too, but they were nothing compared to what my brother had to endure.

Looking back, I realize my mother did try to make things work out between them since her faith in the Lord was so strong. She was very active in the local Lutheran church and even worked as a Sunday school teacher. Once, she even convinced him to attend services with us, but he acted out so badly that she never asked him to attend again.

Finally, on a day that is still so vivid to me, enough was enough. I was ten-years old and they were arguing like they had been doing for months. I sneaked out of my room and watched them from the landing at the top of the stairs. They were really going at it. Next thing I knew, he slapped my mother across her face. The order of events that occurred next are still a blur to me, but what I do know is that within what seemed like minutes, the police were at the door and they were taking my father away.

I remember running back into my room and crying. Mom came upstairs to get me to settle down. She snapped at me in her own unique, tough way, as she wiped my tears. *"What are you crying about?"* I had no answers, just tears. Her gruff approach to soothe us was tough to bear over the years, but I know it was to make us strong.

That image, of my father hitting my mother, has stayed with me throughout my life. If you hit me, there *will* be consequences. My mother clearly taught me that. My parents soon divorced and Dad eventually moved back to his hometown of Brookport, Illinois. It would be another twenty-nine years before Mom, Gordon, and I would see him again.

2

JUST THE THREE OF US (PLUS TWO)

My mom seemed even stronger now since it was just her and us kids. I watched Mom take control of her life and not let anything stop her. Well, almost anything. Remember how I said my mother feared nothing? As it turns out, that assessment was not quite true. My brother and I discovered in our early teens that our mother had this deathly fear of rodents and, of all things, *worms.*

Now, I can understand her disdain for rodents, *"the nasty varmints",* as she called them. Mom believed they lived to race over your feet when you least expected it. She feared them so much that she pulverized my pet hamster that one day he made the mistake of escaping his cage to scurry past her in the kitchen. I watched my five-foot nine-inch tall mother climb on top of a chair and swing away with a vengeance at this two-ounce fur-ball with a broom. While she screeched and cursed at the top of her lungs, I feared for my little pet, but I also grew tickled at the sight of my strong, robust mother terrified of such a little thing. I, too, share her disdain for rodents, but what was it about worms?

Worms really made my mother freeze up. I have never seen anyone so terribly afraid of anything as innocuous as a worm. Be it your standard earthworm variety or your tree-climbing hairy caterpillar, it didn't even matter. Whether it was in the garden, shown on the television, or in a magazine photo, she could not stand the sight of them.

After drenching rainstorms, the earthworms would always venture out and lay all over the sidewalks. Mom refused to leave the house until someone swept off the worms. Even when she was at work, if it rained and the creepy little buggers would slink out onto the walkway, she demanded that someone go outside and clear them off. The woman would not leave work until every last one was gone!

I did ask her why she despised them so.

"They're sneaky!" Mom declared. *"They don't have a face, so you never know what they're up to or what direction they're heading!"* This is also why she declared early on that she didn't want to be buried when she died. *"I can't stand the thought of them crawling all over me!"* You could not reason with her the fact that, being dead, you would not be aware of any of that, but Mom swore up and down, *"I'll know!"* What a funny woman.

Anyway, now that Dad was gone, Mom found a second job. She began working second shift at what they used to call a "State School" (which was more accurately called the State Developmental Center for the Mentally Challenged). She already worked as a beautician on the weekends, using my hair as her guinea pig.

Mom used to hot-comb my hair each week until she realized her efforts were futile with my thick hair. It seems that by the time she had finished with one side of my hair and began to hot-comb the other side, my scalp would sweat so much that my hair would revert to its natural, happy-nappy state. It also didn't help that I would sleep with my head under the covers and sweat out all her work in one day's time.

Mom couldn't wait until I was old enough so she could plaster a relaxer in my hair. Lord, how I hated the smell of that stuff – be it Revlon, or that funky *Vigorol* liquid hair relaxer; it all smelled like rotten eggs to me.

It was also during this time that her two younger sisters moved to Fort Wayne. First to arrive was my Aunt Mable, the "Baby Sister", as they called her. She moved from Phoenix, Arizona, after her divorce and lived with us while Gordon and I were still in elementary school. She was one of the sweetest women you could ever hope to meet.

I recalled once when Mom, Gordon, and I took a long train ride to Phoenix to visit her and our Grandma, who lived with her at the time. We played barefoot outside and chased after the ice cream man, all the while ignoring our feet getting scorched by the hot asphalt.

Grandma and Aunt Mable were so much fun to visit. We always got to help make homemade ice cream in Grandma's old, crank-style churner on their front porch. Now that Aunt Mable was living with us, we knew we would be in for adventure and fun. She never, ever, raised her voice toward us, or anyone else for that matter, and she loved to show us new things. Aunt Mable loved to teach us games, songs, and drive us to Burger King every Friday after school.

Aunt Mable and Mom were total opposites when it came to dispositions. The balance was nice and she was great to live with. A devoted Seventh Day Adventist, Aunt Mable spent her free time with her church, attending prayer meetings and events almost daily. Aunt Mable moved into her own place after a year, once she found work at the local VA Hospital.

Aunt Marie, the middle sister, moved from Chicago and lived with us a few months after her husband passed away. Aunt Marie, who we referred to as the "wild and crazy" aunt, was always up for fun outings and activities. When we were younger, we often took the bus to visit her in Chicago since it was so close to Fort Wayne.

She took us to museums, the local amusement park, and let us stay up late. Aunt Marie took us to ride rickety, wooden roller coasters, and smoked, drank and cursed like a sailor in front of us. Mom said Aunt Marie was always the "fast" one when they were growing up. She was such an extrovert, one who loved to be in your business and tell you what to do.

Nevertheless, Aunt Marie was also an extreme worrier. I could not step out of the house without her being scared that something was going to happen to me. She was truly the opposite of my mother, but that woman could cook! She'd put a serious hurt on you with her flaky peach cobbler, moist oatmeal cookies, drop-off-the-bone turkey and sweet smoked ham.

Shortly after Aunt Marie moved to Fort Wayne, she found employment as a cook - first at a motel and then later at a small residential treatment center for girls. I really envied those girls because my Aunt could fix feasts for them with whatever basic institutional food items she had. When I picked her up from work, the aromas of fried chicken in her clothes and afro-wig made me grin because I knew she had brought some leftovers home with her.

Within another year or two, Aunt Mable bought the house right next door to ours and Aunt Marie moved in with her. Since neither of them had any children, they became our second mothers, and I spent most of my free time at their place until I went off to college.

As for my mother's love life, I honestly cannot recall her ever dating anyone after she and my father broke up. Mom claimed this was because she did not want any man telling her children what to do. She said she was perfectly happy being by herself, and she did not need a man to feel complete. As for the sex, Mom claimed she could live without it.

In truth though, I believe she still held a torch for "Greek". Over the years, Mom would bring him up from time to time, laughing and reminiscing about their good and bad times. She denied still being in love with him, but she did not deny still caring for him, and care she did.

When my older sister, Linda, brought our father back to Fort Wayne in 1996, he was in extremely poor health. Medical reports showed extensive dark matter in his brain from numerous strokes, which resulted in a serious memory loss. He had also been officially diagnosed with schizophrenia. Mom still did not believe what the doctors had to say in this matter, and wished that everyone would just *"leave him be."*

As hard as Linda tried to take care of him and have him live with her, it just became too challenging. He would get up and walk around naked at all hours of the night, soil himself, and say rude, inappropriate things to Linda. For his own safety, Linda thought it best to place him in a nursing home where he could get 24-hour care.

A few days after being placed in a local nursing home, he wandered away from the facility. Hours later, he turned up, of all places, at my mother's house! Mom said he knew that address as "home" and wanted to go where he felt at home. Mind you, this facility was more than ten miles north of Mom's house, and Dad had not been to Fort Wayne for years. Was it love that led him back to Mom's house? Mom denied it, but deep down, I think she thought so.

After that incident, Mom went to visit Dad often in the nursing home and brought him homemade fried chicken and her famous rolls. Every chance she got, she fussed about how there was nothing wrong with "Greek" and that, *"He's just putting everybody on like he used to do."* When he died in 1999, Mom would not go to his funeral because, *"He wouldn't want people staring at him like that."* That woman truly loved that man.

While my parents were together, my mother was determined to make sure we received a good education. She did not want us to attend public school even if that meant we had to travel by bus and were the only black faces in the group. Being members of a Lutheran church, we were eligible to attend any of the local Lutheran schools.

Initially, Concordia Elementary School was within walking distance, being only a few blocks away from our home. I remember spending my first few months there until the school moved to the "suburbs" and my brother and I began riding the bus. As a child, it seemed hundreds of miles away, even though it was only about three miles.

As I grew older, I really did not like being one of only five black students in the entire school amidst a sea of three hundred white students. The only time black folks were talked about was either when our history class spoke of slavery or George Washington Carver. It was embarrassing to hear the white kids chuckle at the slave pictures and then point to me as if that was how all black people looked.

For some reason, Mom never let color issues bother her. She never saw color and often grew angry with black folks who went around blaming all of their misfortunes on "the white man." My mother's strength truly rubbed off on me, because I survived twelve years of that school doing all I could to better myself and become the best person I could be.

Granted, some of my own people within my community, and even some of my relatives, thought I was trying to be "white" because I spoke what they called "proper" English. Look, I had twelve years of English classes and a mother who required we speak respectfully "or else". I make no apologies for my educational upbringing nor do I have regrets. If this is all you know, then that becomes part of who you are.

After my parents divorced, continuing to attend this type of school became financially challenging. Nevertheless, Mom was neither worried nor intimidated. She believed it was our right to attend whatever school she wanted.

Money was tight, but Mom somehow always found a way to pull it off. I recall the days when she took rolls of pennies to the local market to get us bread and bologna to take to school for lunch. Through her perseverance, hard work and sacrifice, she was able to continue sending both my brother and I to private school until we both graduated high school.

Ahh, High School. Not knowing there could only be one queen bee in our "hive", my mother and I always had our share of spats and head-bumping sessions. Whether it was over what I wore or could wear to school, or what time I had to be home after a school event, my mother and I always got into it.

In elementary school, I was pretty good at sneaking questionable clothing past Mom before Aunt Marie came to town. Now, with Aunt Marie around "dipping" her nose into my business, she instigated trouble even before I did anything. My only saving grace was that I was allowed to stay out past dark *only* if I was with my best friend, Tonya. Thank God for Tonya - otherwise I would have never gone anywhere.

Tonya and I have been friends since we were at least seven years old. We lived four houses apart from each other, and although she attended a different Lutheran school, we both ended up attending the same Lutheran high school together. Tonya was the smart, pretty, popular girl. She excelled as a cheerleader, as an editor for the school newspaper, and an actress in the drama club. You name it Tonya *was* it!

When she was on the cheerleading squad, I was on the cheer block team cheering along with them. We both were pretty active in our high school choir and band. She was, and is, a true great friend and we did everything together. From working summer jobs together, flying to California with Aunt Marie, and even liking the same boys, Tonya was my salvation and, to this day, my very best friend. Hanging out with her made me quasi-cool!

Tonya was also my "qualifying" factor when it came to whether I could go somewhere. *"Is Tonya going?"* Mom would ask when I wanted to go to a game or an after-school function. If Tonya was going, then I could go too! This also was true when it came to me being allowed to stay out past sundown. You see, Tonya's house was the place to hang out during the summer. She lived in this huge house with her four siblings and parents, and there was always something going on, whether it was some wonderful cookout or a pool party. Every kid wanted to hang out there.

One thing my mother did not have to worry about with me was boys and sex. By the time we were fifteen, Tonya and I were about the only virgins left in the neighborhood. We were also pretty well developed, much to my Aunt Marie's horror. She would tell Mom I was "fast" but in actuality, I was just lippy with her because I did not like her all up in *my* business.

Mom never seemed to worry about me because she had already put the fear of God in me about pregnancy years earlier. *"If you get pregnant, you're on your own!"* I believed it. Mom also had me believe that kissing boys would get you pregnant. For my sex education, she gave me a book called *The Difference Between Boys and Girls* and then left the room.

She did the same thing years earlier when I was ten and got my period for the first time. Here I was, sitting on the toilet, when she came into the bathroom, gave a me box of Kotex, a rubber band contraption that had metal teeth on it, a book called, *Your Period,* and left the room. That was it.

Unsure as to what to do with the rubber band thing with teeth, I put the pad between my undies and my "private self", like the book said, and went on about my business. It was only after talking to Tonya that I learned the rubber band with the metal teeth was for me to secure around my waist. I was to loop the ends of the maxi pad into the metal teeth. By the time I figured it out, my period was over for the month and my mother never spoke about it again. Let's not even talk about me using tampons. On that subject, I'll just say I spent many a summer on the outside of the pool during "that time of the month."

3

ONLY ONE QUEEN BEE

During my teenage years, hell, during all my life, Mom always had to have the last word. However, the older I became, the more determined I was that I was going to take that honor away from her, if only at least *once*. I soon realized that I was becoming just like her - headstrong and stubborn!

Gordon pretty much minded his own business and got a kick out of our spats. Those two never got into it like she and I did. From my point of view, their relationship was so much softer than ours. Maybe because he was a preemie and not supposed to live; maybe because he was her first born; or maybe because she felt Dad took a lot of his anger out on him and never me.

Whatever the reason, I felt he always got away with everything and I couldn't get away with anything. My brother's curfew was "whenever" but I had to be in the house before it got dark. What a pain in the ass that was during those Indiana winters when it got dark around 5:00 p.m. My brother could hang out and go pretty much anywhere, but I couldn't leave the neighborhood block.

Mom's favorite line to me was *"...Girl, a hard head makes a soft behind!"* Whenever I questioned her authority over me, her other favorite response was *"...Because I'm the Mother!"* Now what kind of sense did that make to a teenager? I suppose that's why I chose to attend an out-of-state college.

After graduating from high school, I attended Indiana-Purdue University at Fort Wayne and worked for a year to get a car. Mom always instilled in us kids that if we wanted something, then we had to work for it. She could not afford to buy me a car, so I saved enough for a down payment. With the help of my older brother, Cletus, who co-signed an auto loan for me, I purchased my first used car.

Now, with my application approved to attend Bowling Green State University, I would finally be going off to college in the fall of 1976. Mom and my aunts took the drive with me to the Ohio school to make sure I got "settled in" – or so they claimed. Mom's last attempt to be "Queen Bee" was to ask for a copy of my dorm room key so that she (or my aunts) could "drop by" and check in on me. Understand, the college was a ninety-minute drive away from Fort Wayne. Why would they be dropping by? Guess who didn't get a copy of the key?

More of our differences came to light during my years away at college. When you're as strong and determined as my mother, you never let anybody tell you that you *can't* do something. Mom was hard-core in this respect - a bit too hard-core for me sometimes.

Mom could never wrap her head around people who got depressed, felt sorry for themselves, or who believed in whatever a doctor or government official said. She would spout, *"Just stop being depressed! What do you have to be depressed about?"* She honestly believed people could just turn on and off their emotions and feelings.

That made it difficult for me to be open with her when I grew distressed over the years, about college, career choices, men, and things I would have loved for her to hear me out on without passing judgment. Her strong, opinionated tactics made me hide many of my feelings from her when I was in my 20s. Not that she was insensitive; I mean she had plenty of compassion and sympathy for the residents at the State Hospital. However, when it came to her own kids, she wanted nothing but strength and positive thinking from us. My mother believed we needed to have the strength within ourselves so we could handle whatever life had to throw at us in the future. I get it now; but then, it would have been nice if she had just a bit more open and understanding.

In 1980, I graduated with a 3.0 GPA from Bowling Green, with my mother and aunts in attendance. Four years of independence was a wonderful thing, and I knew going back into our roles of "dominant-mother" and "compliant-little-girl" was not going to be pretty. You cannot have two *Queen Bees* in the same hive.

Since I turned nineteen, I had been dating a man my mother was not particularly fond of. However, over the course of our six-year relationship, she learned to keep her opinions to herself, at least in front of him. During the summer following my graduation, I hung out at his place and often didn't make it back to my mother's house until midnight. For some reason, that was not acceptable.

One morning, after a night out with him, I discovered that my mother had taken my house key off from my key ring. When I asked Mom why she took it she said, *"If you don't know how to be in the house by the time I go to bed, then you won't get in!"* Now mind you, my mother went to bed at nine, ten o'clock at the latest. Suddenly I was ten-years old again and I could hear her yelling the phrase: *"Be back in this house before it gets dark!"*

For a brief moment, I allowed her to make me feel like I was ten-years-old again, but just for a brief moment. I took a breath and thought here I was, a twenty-four-year-old-3.0- achieving-Who's-Who-in-American-Colleges-and-Universities-winner, now faced with the biggest mother-daughter showdown of my life. Do I let her continue to dominate over me like I was ten-years old, or do I take a stand and behave like the grown young woman that I had become? Lord knows I am my mother's daughter, because in a split-second decision, I turned around, stomped upstairs, packed my bags and moved out.

I think I even surprised my mother with that move. Not ready to move on my own since I had no job yet, I foolishly moved in with my boyfriend, mostly to spite my mother. How's that for mature? Nevertheless, it was necessary and it worked. Mom never treated me like I was ten-years old again – well, at least for a while. Still, since this is not a story about me, I will spare you all the gory accounts of my first failed marriage to that boyfriend, my Mother's inevitable *"...I told you so"*, and my career during that time as a singer and social worker in Fort Wayne. That's another story...

4

THE THREE-DAY CURVE

In 1986, it came as no surprise to my mother when I told her I was going to move to New York to pursue my singing career. Tonya now worked in New Jersey and offered me a place to stay while I auditioned and gave my talents a try. Mom always supported my nightclub gigs, staged musical performances, and the special events I performed in Fort Wayne. I believe she saw herself in me when I made that move, since she struck out as a teenager to do the very same thing. I believe that is why she was against my first marriage. She thought it would stop me from going after my dreams, just like it stopped her from fulfilling her musical dreams.

At first, I worried about my mother being alone, especially since my brother had moved out years earlier. Still, with her sisters living next door, I left feeling mom was going to be okay. She still worked at the state hospital and occasionally did hair. As I think back, I actually don't know why I worried about Mom, because she was always one busy lady.

From her daily trips to the gym, or "spa", as she called it, to her bowling league games, Mom stayed busy. I could barely catch up with her when I made my weekly calls home. Mom loved to swim and then hang out in the steam room after dipping in the ice-cold pool at the spa.

Mom and her sisters also enjoyed long afternoons playing gin rummy, spades, and bid whist. This usually took place on Sundays, when they cooked enough food for an army. As I already noted, my Aunt Marie made the best peach cobbler, with an extra pan of crust made just for dipping in the juices. My Aunt Mable made the best homemade bread and spice cookies that had the perfect amount of spice to make you weep, and, oh my God, my mother made the most heavenly homemade rolls you ever tasted.

Those rolls were the type of Parker House rolls, made from scratch and real butter that melted in your mouth and enticed the entire neighborhood. People would put their order in for Mom's homemade rolls every time she baked them. I would take "care packages" full of zip-locked rolls back to New York with me to eat, and sometimes share, with my friends.

It got so that even my friends put in their orders for me to bring rolls back every time I went home to visit. Mom teased me that that was the first thing I would ask for when I told her I was coming home to visit. Still, she really enjoyed that I, and most of Brooklyn, loved her rolls.

Going to play Bingo with Aunt Marie was another favorite pastime for my mother. I used to accompany them to the smoky Bingo hall when I came home to visit. She called me her "good luck charm." Sure, she would fuss if she lost, but she was also generous with her winnings when she won.

Then there was the traveling. Every summer, until my brother and I moved out, Mom, my aunts, and us kids would hit the road in Mom's Buick and head to Oklahoma to see Grandma. This always coincided with some kind of high school reunion for all three of them to attend, along with a trip to an Indian reservation to play Bingo. Mom and my aunts continued with their annual treks to Oklahoma even after I moved to New York. It was a tradition they loved to experience.

While living in New York, Mom called me like clockwork, every Saturday morning during the Bugs Bunny/Road Runner Hour cartoon show. Although Mom knew I hated to take phone calls during that hour, she called anyway, so we could "watch" the cartoons on the phone together. Even with the time change, somehow the same show was playing on her television as it was on mine.

We'd laugh at the silly Wile E. Coyote and Yosemite Sam, and catch up with each other for the week. On my birthdays, she called during the wee hours of the morning with a bright and cheery, *"Hi, Princess!"* She loved to call me that. With her and my aunts on extensions, they broke into a loud rendition of "Happy Birthday." Reminding her of the time change was futile, because she would proudly profess that she'd been up since *five* and laugh that I was wasting the day away. Our talks were filled with laughter, stories of the past, and updates on folks in Fort Wayne. I really enjoyed our weekly talks, no matter how early she called.

Mom also had the funniest expressions. I would always have to ask her to explain what they meant. For example, when she spoke about my grandma, she'd say, *"Mama's hearing was so good she could hear a rat piss on cotton!"* Don't let her be upset and start talking about how somebody looks or acts. She had the most bizarre descriptions. Like, *"His hair needed combing so bad it looked like rats been suckin' on it"* Or, *"Ooh, Nat, that boy's hair was so beaded up it looked like ants on meat!"* Or, my favorite, *"...she's so stupid she don't know shit from Shineola!"*

Sometimes I thought she was just making them up to get a laugh out of me, but she swore they were true-isms that she heard growing up. Some of the ones I still carry with me are, *"He's as crazy as a road lizard,"* and *"I'll see you tomorrow if the creek don't rise."*

It was during this time I spent in New York that I realized my mother and I were so much alike that we got along better apart than together. I learned that my mother and I had what I called a "three-day curve" with each other. We would get along famously when I came home to visit for days one through three. However, on day four, we would both start fussing with each other and start vying for Queen-Bee-dom! So, I would plan my visits home based on the three-day curve.

My life in New York was turning out pretty good with the touring and jazz clubs I booked. Even when I opted to take a break and use my degree to begin working a "regular job", Mom lovingly supported my choices. I never told her why, but it was because I had a cancer scare. I knew Mom wouldn't understand my feelings of fear even though, after tests and a minor treatment, I was only diagnosed with "abnormal cells" and did not develop cancer.

Mom would not have wanted me to put my life in a doctor's hands, and even though I believed in God and the power of prayer, I could not tell her that I feared getting sick alone in New York with a slew of doctor's bills and without making a real difference to others. Showbiz was cool, but at times it left me empty. Mom would never get it. She would say I had no faith.

When my mother retired from the State Hospital after working there for twenty-five years, I sent her on a cruise to the Caribbean. We worked it out so she could go with her cousin Margaret, who lived in Oklahoma City. I thought Mom would love to swim in the beautiful clear blue waters of the Caribbean, but she had some minor foot surgery earlier in the year and refused to go into the seawater. She honestly believed blood would seep out of her healed incision and lure sharks to attack her! Mom regretted having the surgery, because her foot never felt right since. This only added to her credence to avoid doctors at all costs.

In 1995, I planned to get married for the second, and hopefully, last time, to a wonderful man who turned out to be one of the best things that ever happened to me. The previous year Gregor, my then boyfriend, came home to visit my mother and aunts to officially meet the family and get the "approval" of Ms. Opal Jean.

Despite my own trepidation, Mom and Gregor got along beautifully. She loved the fact that he was a working actor and had also moved to New York from Cleveland, Ohio to follow his dreams. Even more to my surprise, Mom warmly greeted him at the door with a kiss and spoke pleasantly with him. I kept listening for that proverbial "shoe" to drop and within an hour, it did. But even when she threw a barb at him, Gregor caught it, softened it up, and threw it right back at her. He charmed her the way he charmed me – with his sense of humor. That's what she loved about him and made her always have his back.

The spring before we got married, my Aunt Mable suffered her first in a series of strokes. This turn of events really solidified my mother's distrust and disdain for the medical profession. She had Aunt Mable move in with her, as Aunt Marie had moved back to Oklahoma a few years earlier, right before my grandmother died.

Mom looked after Aunt Mable and worked with her to help her get back to where she was before the stroke. The problem was, not everyone reacts the same way to events like the way my mother thinks they should. My aunt suffered moments of sadness about her condition and became sullen. Mom, not being the most sympathetic of people, would become upset with Aunt Mable.

When I called them, they got on both phone extensions for our chat. I would ask Aunt Mable how she was and she would say, *"I guess I'm okay."* Mom would immediately snap at her and say, *"Mable, you need to say you are great, not okay! What is 'okay'?"* This kind of exchange went on and on over the years between the two of them.

My Aunt Mable, being what I can only describe as a saint, never said a harsh word about anyone, let alone my mother, in all the years I've known her. She excused my mother by saying, *"She doesn't mean any harm. She only wants the best for me. I am so grateful for all she's done for me."*

Mom also fought the many doctors who tended to my aunt. Her dislike of them and their tests, medicines, and beliefs caused a lot of bad feelings between them.

My mother's ongoing "...babies and fools" mantra now included *"The only doctor I put my faith in is Dr. God!"* She subscribed to many television evangelists and shared her beliefs with everyone who would listen, and even those who did not want to listen. That was her way.

I learned a lot watching those two interact over the years. My aunt taught me what it meant to be full of grace and understanding of another human being. Perhaps that's what made it so hard to believe anything would ever happen to my mother. Mom told me how she prayed every night for God's protection of her family. She knew that nothing bad was ever going to happen to us, because of her faith in God to look out for us. She instilled in us to never put our faith in any man or doctor; the only one we need to put our faith in is God.

In 2002, Mom and Aunt Mable flew to New York to catch my performance in a one-woman show about Billie Holiday. It was really great having them both visit Gregor and I, since they were not able to visit us years earlier due to Aunt Mable's stroke. Aunt Mable looked frail, but was fully cognizant of what was going on around her. Since I knew how much my mother loved to swim, I set up a swim date for us to go together. While at the gym, I became aware of a strong odor coming from my mother's vaginal area while we sat next to each other in the dressing room.

Thinking that I am now a grown-ass woman, I dared to ask Mom when the last time she had had a Pap smear.

To my surprise, although I guess I should not have been, Mom told me she has not had anyone examine her "down there" since she gave birth to me! Trying not to show my shock, I asked her if she was experiencing any discomfort, irritation, or discharge from her vagina.

Mom quickly said, *"No!"* and proceeded to change the subject. Not wanting to get her any more upset, I dropped the issue.

In hindsight, I should have pressed her about it, but the force that was my mother was greater than anything I have ever come up against.

In 2004, for career purposes, Gregor and I decided to move across the country to California. My mother was surprised, since my life and career had been so good in New York over the past eighteen years. I told her that Gregor had just secured an agent in Los Angeles, and since the 9/11 disaster, there was not much acting work to be had in New York.

Although my day job was secure, the company I worked for was about to initiate some heavy layoffs. Besides, I wanted to support Gregor's dream of trying out California, and I wanted to re-explore my own creative side. Fear had kept me from fully developing my creative skills, and I felt I was ready to create. I had co-written my first screenplay, and it was in an option agreement to be produced.

Despite all my reasoning, deep down I think Mom felt California was much farther away from Indiana than New York, and while she was right, I tried to spin it by telling her that direct flights to Indiana from the west coast were more abundant than flights from New York. Of course, she didn't buy it. In hindsight, maybe she knew she wasn't feeling well. Maybe she didn't want me so far away because I would not be able to be there for her, just in case...

In July of 2004, on our way to California, we stopped in Indiana, sticking to my three-day curve, to visit Mom and Aunt Mable. I noticed that Mom was walking with increased difficulty. Her right knee had bothered her for years, but she always attributed it to arthritis. Mom never really complained about the pain, as to do so, in her eyes, would mean she was embracing the negative, and Mom refused to "own" any negative thoughts.

A creature of habit and not one to spend money on herself, I noticed she still wore a pair of old beat-up sneakers that had to be about five years old. At least that's the last time Mom said she bought herself a pair of sneakers. Mom fought me on it, but Gregor and I took her to get a new pair of orthopedic shoes, hoping that would make her walking less problematic. Mom still believed that if she had not had that foot surgery, her walking would be okay.

Back at the house, Mom smeared Vick's vapor rub on her feet, knees and any other place on her body that ached. When we questioned her about the healing properties of the vapor rub, she testified, *"Laugh if you want, but Vick's really heals!"* She truly believed it could heal her, and she had a supply of those little blue jars with the green top to prove her faith in it.

Our move to California was beautiful and uneventful and Mom knew we would make it there unharmed. After all, she believed in the power of prayer and she had us covered. Mom also believed in our ability to excel in the new challenges that awaited us, as she not only loved me, but she loved Gregor and had faith he would find success in his career in Los Angeles.

5

THE WARNING SIGNS

Early in September 2004, Mom had made the painful decision to place Aunt Mable in a nursing home. Mom told me that on two recent occasions, Aunt Mable had trouble getting up off the sofa when it was time to go to bed. Mom said she tried to help lift her and move her to the bedroom, but was too weak and had been unable to do so. Fearful of dropping her, Mom left her on the sofa for the evening.

During the night, Aunt Mable had somehow been able to maneuver herself up and into her bed. Of course, that made Mom think Aunt Mable was faking it. I told her Aunt Mable would not fake something like that and she needed to be more patient with her. I again asked her to take my previous advice to hire a full-time nurse to come in and help out since Mom was getting so frustrated. Aunt Mable had great private insurance from her years working for the VA hospital, so nothing would come out of pocket. Mom was against it. She did not feel "strangers" in her home would look out for Aunt Mable, especially when Mom wasn't home. She feared they would just rip her off. She felt the same way about nursing homes.

Mom could not understand why Aunt Mable would not practice her physical therapy at the house, especially when the PT (physical therapy) nurse would come by and work with her on it. Mom believed if she worked on her therapy, she would not have problems getting around. Frustrated, Mom accused Aunt Mable of being "negative" and told her she should try to get up on her own. Deep down, my mother believed my aunt could move, but just wanted attention.

When Mom acted this way, Aunt Mable naturally became upset and asked to go to the hospital. This went on for a couple of months, but when I tried to intervene, Mom snapped at me and accused me of "babying" Aunt Mable. Mom still held onto the notion that everyone should be as strong and positive as she was. She refused to believe that Aunt Mable could be suffering from depression and loneliness.

Honestly, I believe my aunt did grow lonely at the house, because Mom often went out to play bingo, went to the "spa", and visited her cousin Mildred's house so often. Mom was sometimes harsh with my Aunt in this respect, but her usual "tough love" technique was failing this time.

When I spoke to Aunt Mable about it, she always defended Mom. *"Opal don't mean no harm..."* Auntie would say in her sweet way. *"You know she hasn't been feeling well, but she'll never admit to it."* When I asked what she meant, Aunt Mable said

Mom's knee has really been bothering her. I believe Aunt Mable actually thought she was a burden to Mom.

I know Mom never felt that way. In fact, she often grew angry with Aunt Mable when she thanked her for being there for her. *"What are you thanking me for? I'm supposed to be there for you!"* Mom would snap. Mom really needed to work on her warm and fuzzy bedside manner.

After a few trips to the ER and nothing was found wrong with my aunt, Mom became increasingly weary of my Aunt Mable's requests to leave. She felt that perhaps she was wrong in her initial thoughts about nursing homes and that, maybe, full-time assisted care would be best for Aunt Mable. Mom had always been dead-set against placing family in a nursing home because she believed abuse and neglect ran rampant in those facilities.

But Mom also feared that one day she would attempt to move Aunt Mable, and that, with her bad knee, they would both fall and neither one would be able to get up and get help. My aunt's physician even mentioned to Mom that he was concerned with them living together, since they both had ambulatory difficulties. Of course, Mom just thought the doctor was trying to bilk my aunt's insurance for more money and ignored him.

In November 2004, my aunt became a resident of the Applewood Nursing Facility. Mom swore she would be there every day to make sure "no sneaky shit" was going on there. Mom would tell the staff, *"You all will never know when I'll tip up in here! There better not be any marks on her either!"*

Mom was true to her words. The facility was small, and Aunt Mable shared a room with one other person. The place had a wide gambit of daily activities from sing-along's (my Aunt's favorite), to outings at restaurants, to weekly bingo, crafts, as well as physical and occupational therapy. Aunt Mable said she was happy with the facility, and her church family visited daily.

Since my husband and I had just moved to the west coast, there was no way we could make it home for the Thanksgiving holiday. Mom understood and jokingly promised to send me some of her famous homemade rolls through the mail. Mom still called to tease me when she was making those mouth-watering rolls. She would slowly chew on one and playfully offer to send me one "through the telephone." She did that a lot, especially during the wintertime. Whenever the first snow fell in Fort Wayne, she would call me, no matter how early, and tell me about it. She asked if I wanted her to put some in the freezer and save some. I always called her bluff, which made us both laugh.

Up until Thanksgiving 2004, Mom called every Sunday or Saturday morning, bright and early, regardless of the time change, to catch up like we always did. She'd sometimes even be brazen and say, *"Good morning, Princess! Were you and my favorite son-in-law making babies?"* She would never say sex, even at that stage in our lives. I would get embarrassed, but Gregor would take the phone and jokingly say to her, *"...as a matter of fact..."* and start laughing. They both got a kick out of torturing me.

However, this particular Thanksgiving, I sensed something was not quite right with Mom. She said she had not been able to go swimming at her "spa" because her hip and leg had been bothering her. She blew it off as arthritis and said she would spend her day with Aunt Mable at the nursing home.

We spoke more often than usual during the next few weeks. Mom continued to complain that her hip and leg were bothering her. I kept urging her to see a doctor, but of course, Mom wasn't having that. She was content to steam herself in a hot bath and rub herself down with some vapor rub.

On Christmas morning, we had not heard from Mom and it was already past 8:00 a.m. I knew this was odd, so we called her. Mom really sounded annoyed. She said that she believed she had pulled a muscle in her hip or groin area and was having a hard time sleeping because of the pain. I could not believe my mother actually admitted to having pain! I knew something was seriously wrong.

I strongly urged her to go to the emergency room, or to schedule a visit with her doctor. Of course, she refused, especially since she had no real doctor to go to. She said the only doctor she would see was Dr. Wilson, the man who brought me into the world, but he was long-since deceased. I urged her to please consider the emergency room, but Mom hated waiting just about as much as she hated doctors. She felt the waiting would be more painful to her than the pain in her hip. She opted to take a long hot bath and then would rub her hip down with some vapor rub and ice. She believed that would work, if it were just a pulled muscle.

I got up especially early on New Year's Day 2005 to call Mom, but this time she was very subdued and not as upbeat as usual. I asked her what was wrong, and she said she was still in pain. She got me off the phone quickly, claiming she was going to get into the tub – but it was only 11:00 a.m., her time. Again, I knew something was seriously wrong.

Sure, I was worried about my Mother, but I also knew she was stronger than any woman I had ever known. I just *knew* she was fine…or was going to be fine.

On a sunny Sunday, January 8, 2005 I had just got back from walking our dog when Gregor told me that Mom had called. He said Mom was letting us know she had just come back from the emergency room. She had gone due to her pain.

I immediately called Mom back, but she sounded out of it. She told me that Cousin Mildred had taken her to the emergency room at Parkview Hospital. After waiting what she defined as "forever", the doctor completed his examination and told her she had gout. He gave her a shot of morphine and two prescriptions: one was for Darvocet-N for pain, and Indocin for the gout.

"Gout? What the hell is gout?" I asked her. "And since when do doctors give out morphine shots like they're flu shots?" Something was not right about all of this.

Mom said the reason she sounded so groggy was because she had taken *two* of the Darvocet pills about an hour ago, on top of the morphine shot. I told Mom that this was not a wise thing to do, especially because she sounded so loopy. Mom admitted she might have overdone it, but the pain was so unbearable. She now wanted to take a nap, so I told her I would check up on her later.

After I hung up, I called Cousin Mildred to see exactly what was going on. Cousin Mildred, long-time cousin and "best friend" of Mom and her sisters, sounded really concerned about

Mom. She also admitted that Mom must have been in some sort of pain to endure the madness of a hospital emergency waiting room. I asked Mildred to please look in on her, as I explained how Mom got heavy-handed with the meds and was sounding so out of it.

The next day, I called Mom early to check in on her. She did sound much better, not as groggy. She also realized that she should not have taken two of those pain pills on top of that morphine shot. She promised to be more careful with the remaining pills, but she was really still in a lot of pain.

Mom also disclosed that she'd lost about fifty pounds – without trying - over the past few months, and had not had a bowel movement in over a week!

"What do you mean, you lost all that weight without trying?" I questioned. I was really worried now. What in the world was going on with my mother?

6

NOT GETTING ANY BETTER

I decided it was time to call my brother, Gordon, who lived in Columbus, Ohio, to let him know what was going on with Mom. Gordon called me back after first speaking with Mom, and said she'd told him it was nothing but gout. I told him I did not think she really had gout and would do some research online.

After speaking with him, I called Mom to check in on her. She was annoyed that I told Gordon that she was sick and in the hospital. I responded that "technically", she was in the hospital and tried to laugh it off. She admitted she had been glad to hear from him, since Gordon was not prone to calling any of us as often as I would like. He would call once or twice a year, tops. Mom was always okay with that and never complained, nor held it against him.

Later that evening, I searched the Internet about gout. Apparently, the condition affects the feet, fingers, and knees, but rarely the spine. Nowhere did it indicate that it affects the hip or groin area. Also, the information indicated that the test to diagnose gout was performed by withdrawing fluid out of the affected joint with a needle. I knew full well Mom did not undergo this type of examination.

The following day, I again called to check in on Mom. She sounded much better and said she was still in pain but had been able to sleep the last couple of nights with the medication. I told her what I found on the Internet about gout and asked what kind of test the doctor performed on her last week. She indicated he only did an x-ray of her hip.

A couple of days later, on the morning of my birthday, Mom called as she always did, bright and early, to wish me a happy birthday. It was 7:00 a.m., my time, but even through my sleepy haze I could tell that Mom didn't sound good at all. She didn't even try to sing to me like she usually did. Her *"Good morning, Princess"* greeting lacked its usual joy and brightness. Mom denied feeling out of sorts and quickly got me off the phone.

The next day, I called her, early in the morning. She sounded like she was in pain and disclosed that she did not sleep at all the previous night due to the severity of the pain in her groin. Cousin Mildred was there and intended to take her back to the emergency room at Parkview to get some more pain pills, since she was out.

I told her that this has gone on long enough and she needed to check herself into the hospital to find out what was really going on. Both Mildred and I pointed out that she was not getting any better and could barely walk. Mom argued that she did not want to check herself into the hospital, as she hated doctors - they only make you sicker, etc., etc. I told her that if she did not check herself in, I would be on a flight to Ft. Wayne today. She fussed that I could not leave my job, since I just started working at a new job, but we argued back and forth until Mom finally agreed to let Mildred take her.

In speaking to Mildred later, I found out they did have to call an ambulance to get her, as Mom could not stand up, yet alone walk. Mildred also told me they took another x-ray, and an MRI, and it showed Mom had a cracked hip! What a relief to finally have an answer to the source of Mom's pain. I was glad Mildred forced Mom to go to the hospital – now she could get the help she needed. Mildred told me the doctor was going to admit her, complete further work-ups, and perform surgery the following morning at 11:00 a.m.

I called Gordon and left messages as I continued to get updates on Mom. I also called my sister, Linda, who lived in Fort Wayne, and told her everything that happened. She also had been talking to Mom and felt she did not have gout. I told her Mom always downplayed her ailments due to the fact that she hated doctors. Linda said she would go visit her at the hospital the following day, and I told her I would be in town later that week.

The next morning, I attempted to call Mom at the hospital, but they had already taken her down to surgery. I then contacted Linda, who said she would call me once the surgery was completed. Of course, I was confident everything was going to be all right because it was just a broken hip. Mom was strong and has always maintained a positive attitude.

I laughed to myself just thinking about how much grief Mom would give the doctors about wanting to be released once her surgery was completed. When Linda called me back, she reported that Mom was in recovery and that the doctor had put a rod in her hip to help with healing. The tone in Linda's voice then began to change, and I knew there would be a "now here's the bad news" comment.

Apparently, the doctors did find something wrong with Mom's hipbone and they were going to perform a biopsy, along with a CAT scan. Linda explained that the doctor intended to call in a cancer specialist to look everything over. They would have the results in two days, which would be Wednesday. I assured Linda that I would be in town by then. Linda gave me the names and phone numbers of the five doctors and Cancer Services Client Advocate that had been assigned to Mom's case.

Damn, I thought, as she read them off. *Why so many doctors if nothing's wrong?* I told myself to breathe. *Nothing has been proven yet, and doctors make mistakes. Hell, they don't know everything. Mom is strong. Mom CAN'T have cancer!* I closed my eyes as these thoughts swam through my head.

My heart sank as I allowed the negative aspect of these thoughts to enter my mind. *What the hell? Stop thinking the worst! What would Opal Jean say if she saw you like this? Just stop it!* The phone was still in my hand, and I took a breath and called Mom's room. Mom sounded groggy from the surgery. I didn't keep her long, just enough to tell her I loved her. I also didn't tell her I was on my way to Fort Wayne, as I knew she would fuss with me about it. Afterward, I called the hospital and was connected to the nurse's station on Mom's floor, and spoke with her nurse, who told me she was recovering fine from the hip surgery.

The next morning, I called Mom. She sounded more alert but was still in a bit of pain. She joked with me and put on a good front, but I could sense she was tired. I was glad that Linda was also there visiting Mom when I called. Linda and my Mother had always shared a special relationship.

It was no big deal to Mom that our father was first married to Linda's mother. Mom always embraced Linda and brother Cletus, and treated them like they were her own. So, I was grateful that Linda took on the challenge of being there with Mom when I was so far away in California. I knew she had just lost her mother the year before, so I knew this could only be painful for her.

Linda shared that the doctor was drawing blood and running more tests. She also explained that Mom's white blood count was low, so they gave her blood during the surgery. I told Linda to refrain from telling Mom that I would be there tomorrow as she'd only get upset and argue that I needed to stay in California and "keep my new job". Linda told me that it was too late, as the nurse had already told Mom I was coming. At that point, I heard Mom fussing at me in the background about, *"You're gonna lose your job!"*

Linda handed me back to Mom and I pretended not to have heard what she said. I only laughed and told her I loved her. Mom continued to fuss. *"You promised you wouldn't come if I went to the hospital. You're gonna lose your job!"* I fussed back that I could *always* get another job, but I only had *one* mother. I also told her that Gordon was aware that she was in the hospital and had told me he would be coming up from Columbus by Friday. Even in her tired state, she tried to argue me about this, but deep down I knew she wanted to have us there.

In my heart, I wasn't so sure Gordon would really come. As much as I loved my brother, he was not one to keep in touch or pick up the phone on holidays and birthdays, let alone travel three hours to visit home. Mom always excused Gordon's lack of calling and staying in touch *"because he's a boy."* Another one of her beliefs that always nagged at me was that Mom had accepted that this was just Gordon's way and that no news was good news. However, if I failed to call weekly, she would be upset because, according to Mom, it's "expected" of girls to stay in touch.

The morning of January 19, 2005 I left sunny California early and arrived late to a gray and cold Fort Wayne. A carpet of snow lay on the ground, and I thought it looked so peaceful and lovely. I arrived at the hospital around dinnertime. Mom looked good, considering what she'd been through. She had clearly lost a lot of weight since I last saw her in August, and her arm was a bit bruised from the IV, but she seemed upbeat and happy to see me. I could see the pain in her eyes from her broken hip as she tried to work in a *"Didn't-I-tell-you-not-to-come?"* argument. I hugged her gently and kissed her on the forehead as I told her to hush.

I asked if Dr. Carr had come by today with the test results and Mom said he had not. She then quickly changed the subject to Linda, who had stopped by but left a while ago to go to work. Since Mom clearly didn't want to talk about the test results, we tapped-danced around small talk. *"How was my husband?... How was the flight?... How was the traffic with all that snow?"* Mom never really could deal with troubling issues, especially if it involved her. So, I gave her that moment, for now, and danced the dance with her.

We caught up for about three hours before I left to go to Mom's house, the house I had grown up in, for the night. I told Mom I would be back bright and early in the morning after I visited Aunt Mable in the nursing home.

Visiting Aunt Mable the next morning was even more difficult than I had anticipated. It appeared clean and the staff was pleasant, but there's just something about those facilities and that smell...medicinal, age-filled, odors of old folks just waiting. Waiting to be visited, waiting to be changed, waiting to be fed ...waiting to die. I never wanted this for Aunt Mable. I know Mom must have been feeling out of sorts to have her placed in a nursing home.

I was led to the dining area where Aunt Mable was asleep in her wheelchair. She really looked good; peaceful, but worn. I felt pleased to see her hair was neatly brushed and her clothing was clean. I gently woke her and she gave me that unforgettable smile that just lit up the room. She told me she knew Mom was in the hospital and said she cried when she first heard about it. She said she now knows that Mom is going to be fine and home in no time.

Aunt Mable's face was bright and cheery and her attitude was positive and hopeful. She even joked for me to tell Mom, *"She better get well and get her butt home!"* We laughed and I told her I would pass on her message and that I would be back to visit every day while I was in Fort Wayne. I gave her the biggest kiss and hug before leaving and heading over to visit Mom. I did speak briefly to the nursing home's social worker, and informed her that Mom was hospitalized. Any questions or issues they had regarding Aunt Mable should be directed to me.

7

THE DIAGNOSIS...AND THE
ELEPHANT IN THE ROOM

Overnight, the snow had frozen so the roads were icy. Traveling to the hospital was usually a fifteen-minute ride from the nursing home, but this morning took about an hour due to the weather. God, how I missed California. Fortunately, Parkview Hospital makes it a point to keep their parking lots and sidewalks clear so maneuvering inside their facility was not a problem.

Mom was just coming back to her room from physical therapy when I arrived. She looked tired, but she pushed right through it. Mom is one tough lady. She maintained her sense of humor even though I could see the pain she was in. I asked if Dr. Carr had been by yet and Mom told me he had not, but the nurse said they were waiting on me to get there before calling him in. I went to find the nurse who put the call in to Dr. Carr, and we were told he would be in to speak with us around 1:00 p.m.

Mom put on that she was not worried about the meeting with Dr. Carr, but I could tell she was just trying not to worry me. She asked about Aunt Mable and turned on her television so she could catch up with her "stories", a.k.a. the soaps. Janet, the hospital social worker, came by to discuss Mom's continued care for rehabilitation for her broken hip. She talked about what type of care she might need and where it would take place. Of course, she said such issues would depend on possible additional treatment challenges, if any, Mom would have to deal with after we heard from Dr. Carr.

Mom was polite to Janet, but didn't say much to her during the discussion. As it grew closer to 1:00, Mom grew a bit more anxious. Among Mom's many reasons to dislike doctors was that they always keep you waiting. *"If I'm on time, then they should be on time!"* Mom used to fuss. However, Dr. Carr was right on time.

A serious, older man, Dr. Carr wasted no time getting to the issue at hand. I turned off the television, much to Mom's dismay, and we both avoided looking at each other while Dr. Carr spoke. He reported that the surgeon had noticed abnormalities with the appearance of Mom's hip during the surgery and had performed a biopsy, along with ordering a CAT scan. The biopsy and CAT scan revealed that Mom had lymphoma, a cancer of the lymph nodes.

Dr. Carr went on to explain that this type of cancer is usually first detected in the lymph nodes; however, in Mom's case, the cancer has spread to her hipbone, her liver, and her lungs. They had also discovered that Mom had a new lump in the side of her throat and believed the cancer had spread there as well. Dr. Carr stated that he was aware that Mom was against any type of chemotherapy treatment, so he offered all treatment options open to her.

Mom was quiet and unemotional. I was falling apart inside, but I concentrated my focus on Dr. Carr's face and the words he spoke. I kept waiting for him to say, *"There's no need to worry, there's a cure"*... or *"Your Mom will be fine with a little radiation"* ... anything other than what he was saying. Dr. Carr only offered the following options for Mom to consider:

- Do Nothing. The cancer will continue to grow and consume her hip, liver and lungs. Mom will experience more breaks in her bones as well.
- Undergo radiation therapy on the tumor in her hip only, but this will shrink that mass only; they could then begin to treat other tumors.
- Begin daily chemo pill/oral therapy. This will attack most cells, including the non-cancerous ones in her body. Hair loss would be minimal; Mom would experience nausea and weakness and pills would need to be taken daily.
- Undergo 6 treatments of full IV chemotherapy; one session every three weeks. This would be done in conjunction with other treatments to limit side effects. Chemo would be done as a walk-in to his office. The treatment would cause hair loss, nausea, vomiting, and weakness.

It was a lot to drink in but I struggled to remain as calm as possible. I asked about radiation for all the tumors, but Dr. Carr said that type of treatment, while it would work well on the tumor in her hip, does not work as effectively on soft tissue and would not be helpful to Mom.

Mom was quiet, and I knew she was trying to put on a strong face. Dr. Carr said he would be available to answer any further questions, but did state that he would have to extract some of Mom's bone marrow before beginning any treatment and that could be done at his office. He also wanted us to meet with the radiologist to start treatment on the tumor in Mom's hip.

After he left, Mom turned the TV back on and acted as if nothing had been said. *Okay, now what?* I thought. Do I say nothing and let her drink it in, or do I open my mouth and start crying like the big baby I'm feeling like inside? Neither one of us wanted to discuss the elephant, now lurking in the room.

A few moments passed, and without looking up from the television, Mom asked me what should she do? She's asking *me?* No one tells Mom what to do, let alone suggest a course of treatment she's totally against. Knowing how Mom felt regarding doctors and cancer treatments, I took a deep breath, held in my emotions, and told Mom it should be totally up to her. Still, knowing how much she loved being able to move about, I added that she might feel better if we treat the hip problem *first* so she could at least walk and even go swimming again.

Mom appeared open to that. I told her that we could continue to explore her options and question what was fully involved with the other proposed treatments and go from there. Mom broke eye contact with the television, ever so briefly, looked at me, and agreed to the radiation. She looked back at the television and then said she would put it in God's hands. She said she would rather try the pill therapy because she did not want her activities limited if she took the full chemo treatment.

We continued to pretend to watch the television for another twenty minutes, and Mom only spoke during commercials, mainly about the commercials. After a little while, Janet, the social worker, returned. She informed us that the hospital had a bed for Mom in their continued care unit on the 5th floor. Mom would be moved the following day.

I hung out all day with Mom. I took a brief break to get a salad in their café and used that time to call Linda, Tonya, and Gregor. I also took that break to cry a bit over the news. They all were great and supportive. I asked Gregor to call my job and tell them that I had a family emergency and would not be back next week. Being such a private person, Mom asked me to not tell any of her friends or family about the cancer. Really? Not even Gordon, I asked? Not even Gordon. Nevertheless, I knew, and so did she, that I was going to call him this evening.

Back at Mom's house, I went into work-mode and researched the hell out of this disease on my laptop. I realized that Mom had, *"Type Four Lymphoma…the type that has spread to two or more organs…"* - check. *"…typically this disease stays in the lymph nodes and can be eradicated with radiation."* – check. *"…*

when it's in the surrounding tissues it must be attacked with full chemotherapy…" – check.

It also noted that, *"…if it's in the liver, surgery could be done to remove the tumor as this organ regenerates itself."* – check. I needed to ask Dr. Carr about that and to what extent Mom's liver and lungs were affected. I further learned that Mom's *"…lack of appetite is caused by the damage to the liver since this organ aids digestion and filters out poisons in the blood…"* – check, *check, fuckin'* check! Suddenly I'm overcome with anger, hurt, tears, and loss of control. *"Stop it, Nat"*, I muttered, but I couldn't breathe, I couldn't see straight, my heart was breaking and I couldn't do a damn thing about it. *"Fuck! What is wrong with you? You need to be as strong as your mother!! Stop it!"* Damn, I wish I had a drink.

The house was too somber and quiet. So much of it had remained the same since I had grown up here; current and old TV Guides on the sofa, coffee maker holding a carafe of day-old coffee, bills on the coffee table to be paid. So empty, just the house and me. I called American Airlines and cancelled my Sunday flight home. I wiped my tears, took a breath and resumed work-mode, setting up tasks to attend to since I was going to be in Fort Wayne for a while. I unpacked my winter clothes I left here when we moved from New York to California. So glad I did, as it was freezing here.

I put a call in to Gordon and left a message, then spoke with Hubby and checked in on him and our dog. I chatted with my sister, Linda and best buddy Tonya, keeping busy, keeping busy…keeping busy…until 2:00 a.m. Then, I crawled into Mom's bed and stared at the beam of light coming in from the street peeking through her curtains. The last time I checked, her bedside clock said it was 4:00 a.m.

I awoke later, swollen faced, chilly, and exhausted – it was only 5:30 a.m.? Ugh! I knew I could not continue like this. I needed to shake off this funk and face this day with the hope and determination that God would get us through this and would take care of everything. I took a quick shower, made a call to Aunt Mable's nursing home, and stopped at a local bakery to pick up a breakfast croissant for Mom on my way to the hospital. It's amazing how many folks are up and about in Fort Wayne on a chilly, icy, Friday morning.

When I arrived at the hospital, the staff were just bringing Mom to her room from physical therapy. She appeared tired and had already eaten some of her breakfast, but still managed to take a few bites of the sandwich I brought. Mom was quiet and told me I looked tired. I joked, *"You've got your nerve!"* and she gave me a brief smile. Mom said the radiologist had come by earlier, but would return once I arrived.

No sooner than she spoke those words when in walked Brenda, the radiology nurse. She told us that their facility was down the street from the hospital, and they provide transportation for Mom's treatment sessions. Brenda said they would begin radiation treatments after Mom's scheduled January 28th surgery to fix the hip, and the sessions would last fourteen days. Radiation treatment would take place daily in order to shrink the tumor in her hip and decrease pain levels so Mom would be more comfortable. I told Brenda that we needed to speak again with Dr. Carr about setting up the bone marrow extraction, since Mom was still in the hospital. She said she would contact his nurse.

After Brenda left, Mom seemed a bit more hopeful about the radiation treatment. Apparently, she thinks all the tumors would be gone after the radiation. Mom has always been the ultimate optimist and far be it from me to tell her not to have faith, but I did remind her that Dr. Carr said that radiation would most likely only take care of the one tumor in her hip. Mom did say she remembered, but added in her own unique way, *"Doctor's don't know everything!"* Lord, how that woman makes me laugh!

Even facing all this drama, Mom still wants to refute what the doctor has to say. I did dare to ask Mom if she thought any more about the type of chemo she wanted to explore. Surprisingly, Mom seemed to warm up to the full I-V treatment option, even if it included losing her hair. Imagine that!

We hung out together pretty much all day. Around 3:30 p.m., her new room was ready and the staff moved Mom and all her belongings to Room 516, Bed 1. I tucked Mom in after dinner and left for the day. Before I left, I saw that Mom needed some things, so I headed to K-Mart and picked up some underwear. Heavy snow greeted me as I left the store's parking lot. It picked up quickly as I made my way back to Mom's house.

At the house, I packed up some of Mom's favorite sweat pants and her bowling tee shirt for wearing to physical therapy, along with her nightgown. I made another call to Aunt Mable's nursing home to check on her and then crashed early into Mom's bed.

8

SNOW, EUCALYPTUS AND PEPPERMINT OIL ADDED TO THE MIX

Saturday, January 22nd through January 24th, 2005

The heavy, wet snowstorm that started the day before continued into the following morning. It looked like eight inches was already on the ground, with another eight still expected today. I called Mom around 7:00 a.m. and told her about the snow. She told me to stay off the road because folks drive so crazy in Fort Wayne. I asked how she was feeling; of course, I knew she was hurting as I could hear it in her voice. Mom admitted to being in a lot of pain but she was putting up with it. She quickly changed the subject to ask me about Aunt Mable, Gregor, the house, and her bills. I told her when I come to the hospital tomorrow, I would bring her workout clothes and her nightgown.

Mom and I chatted about three more times that day. She went on and on about various things, happy to have finally had her third bowel movement this week. Mom also noted her appetite had improved and ate a bit more of her meals today. She sounded happier the last time we spoke today. I hate to admit it, but it was good to have a break from the hospital, though I felt guilty for not being able to make it to see Mom and Aunt Mable.

Later that evening the snow finally stopped, but the damage was done – a foot of drifting snow and plenty of ice. I dug out my rental car and moved it across the street so the city plows could clear off the snow. I tried to do some laundry, but Mom's washer has ongoing "issues" so I ended up cleaning the house and making note of things she would need once she was released to come home.

Mom called at 8:00 a.m. bright and early the next morning. I was just waking up, but lied and said I had been up for a while. She quickly informed me that she heard the roads were clear, which was my cue to say I would be at the hospital shortly after re-digging myself out. The winds had really kicked up last night and there was still a lot of snow drifting.

By 9:00 a.m., I was dressed and out the door, shovel in hand. I re-did the steps, sidewalk, and my car. Have I mentioned how much I missed California? Two drifts of foot-high hardened snow had effectively fenced in Mom's car. There was no digging it out. Fortunately, the sun was out, and it was supposed to warm up, not only today, but also during the week. I should be able to dig her out then. I climbed into my rental car and headed out.

On the way to the hospital, I stopped by the nursing home to see Aunt Mable. Their parking lot was slushy and slick. *What the hell?!* They have frail senior citizens here – you'd think they'd make it a priority to plow and salt their lot. Once safely inside, I found Aunt Mable sitting in her wheelchair with her coat on.

Auntie was happy to see me and told me she had her coat on because she was "a bit cool." Aunt Mable was in good spirits and quite chatty with me. She asked about Gregor and our dog, Zorro – she loved our little Jack Russell Terrier. I avoided talking about Mom, but Aunt Mable kept bringing her up. She knew I was hiding something and her expression began to fall. She appeared sad, so I only told her that Mom had broken her hip (a truth) and that she would be in the hospital for a while.

Aunt Mable still looked sad, so I pulled out my cell phone and called Mom so they could talk to each other. The two have not talked since Aunt Mable moved to her new room, which had no telephone. It was sweet hearing them talk to each other. Aunt Mable fussed at Mom and told her to listen to the doctors and to get better. It was clear that they really needed to talk to each other, especially on Mom's side, since she'd been feeling guilty about not being able to visit Aunt Mable. The entire visit was quite emotional for all of us, and it was difficult to leave my aunt. She was so sweet and fragile. I had decided not to tell Aunt Mable about Mom's real health issues, as I knew it would destroy her emotionally.

I made it to Mom's bedside around 10:30 a.m. She actually looked good – much better than the last time I'd seen her. Mom said her pain was still pretty intense, and the nurse had removed the dressing around the staples at the incision site on her hip. Mom wore knee-high orthopedic compression stockings to prevent blood clots and complained how tired she was of wearing them.

I showed Mom the bag of clothing I had brought, along with some aromatic eucalyptus peppermint oil, which I knew she loved. I rubbed some on her legs and arms and massaged them, much to Mom's delight. She smiled and looked a bit more relaxed as I continued the rubdown.

Mom was in a talkative mood and began to run down the usual memories from my childhood to her roommate. Mom so loved telling folks about my childhood antics and adolescent ways. I soon changed the subject by pulling out the bills she asked me to bring, along with a get-well card from her friends at her "spa" that really made her day.

We spread out the bills, both hers and Aunt Mable's, and we separated them into "pay now" and "pay later" piles. Mom insisted that I bring both her and Aunt Mable's checkbook so *she* could write out the checks. I get it. Although she knows I am more than capable of writing out the checks and mailing the bills, she wants to feel like she's still in control.

After about an hour, I asked her what she wanted me to do for her and what her expectations were from this point. I also wanted to broach the subject of the radiation that would commence that week. Short of her worrying about me losing my job by being here "too long", Mom said she wanted to give me her power of attorney.

What the hell? Why would she want me to have this kind of control? What happened to the "everything's-gonna-be-alright" mindset?

Mom continued to shock me by telling me she didn't want her life prolonged by artificial means if all attempts to save or revive her ever occur. *I don't want to hear this, Mom, please!* I thought. Outwardly, I remained calm. Mom looked pretty cool saying all of this to me, and said she wanted me to take care of her affairs as if they were my own.

Then, she grew silent. I couldn't speak for what seemed like forever. When I finally spoke, I told her I planned on staying in Fort Wayne until the chemo began. I knew she would object to this, which she did, so I had my "back-up plan", which I also knew she would object to, standing by. I told her when I did leave, I would only do so if I hired a visiting nurse to come to her house at least three times a week to help her out.

Lord have mercy, why did I bring that up? Mom grew totally upset with that option. *"Under no circumstances do I want any stranger lurking around my house!"* Mom exclaimed. She could take care of herself without *anybody's* help! She also threw in that her cousin, Mildred, who was also older and has some health issues, could come by and help her out. And how dare I suggest she could not take care of herself, how dare I suggest such negativity! Okay, okay, I knew that would be her answer. I would let her win this one… for now. Nevertheless, I told her I was still not going back until I felt comfortable, so she had to pick one or the other.

I quickly changed the subject, although I secretly enjoyed watching her getting riled up - it was good seeing her back to her old self. I couldn't take any more of that living-will talk. Mom resorted to flicking on the television so we could focus on something other than our conflict. We ended up watching *Misery*, with James Cann. Of course, Mom wanted to know what was going to happen before it happened, talking all through the movie. That is one funny lady.

Lunch soon arrived, which was awful – some pale-ass broccoli, an undercooked baked potato, and turkey with cold gravy... ugh! Mom did try to eat some of the food, but I could tell she was really pissed off at the meal. She soon threw up her hands and just sat there. She had mentioned earlier that she had a taste for some fish. I asked her if she still wanted some. She was too frustrated to make a decision, so I told her I would be back shortly.

I left the room to call my sister, Linda, to see where we could get some good fried fish. She knew of some fast food fish joints on the other side of town from the hospital, but nothing too close. I ended up going down to the hospital café, and as it turned out, they had fried fish – and not too bad, either. I got Mom two pieces and a Sprite. She was still pretty hungry and ate over half of one of the pieces. After that, Mom's spirits got better, and we continued our afternoon watching bowling on TV and then I combed her hair.

Linda came by around 3:30 that afternoon and hung out with us for a while. It was only during that visit that it occurred to me that Mom had not gone to the bathroom since early that morning. I needed to see her walk and go pee. Mom called the nurse, who came very quickly, as Mom tends to try and walk on her own despite being told not to. That's my Mom. She did pretty well with her walker and was able to make it to the bathroom instead of the bedside potty. It was good to see her moving about. Afterward, she wanted to sit up for a while.

Linda and I hung out for another twenty minutes and then we left. I had not eaten all day and was starving. Linda and I went out to dinner and then I went back to Mom's house.

I checked in on Mom around 8:00 p.m. to see if her dinner had been any better than lunch. She said her meal wasn't too bad and even ate about half of it. We chatted about ten minutes as she drifted off to sleep. I wished her sweet dreams. Mom really sounded so frail for the first time since all this began.

First thing the next morning, I went into "task mode," first calling Dr. Carr's office to get answers to additional questions I had concerning Mom's tumors. His office said he'd be out until Tuesday, but they would make sure he called me. Check. I then contacted Sears repair to have someone come out to fix her bloody washing machine. Someone could come out Wednesday between 1:00 and 5:00 in the afternoon. It would cost $55.00, which would be applied as a credit to the bill if I let him repair it. Check. I also contacted AAA to set up Mom's car inspection for her new insurance policy with them – they could see me anytime between 9:00 and 5:00 that day. Check, check, check.

I arrived at the hospital around 10:30 a.m. Cousin Mildred was there, and she and Mom were already watching the soaps. Mom looked quite good, although she fussed about her physical therapy, which she had just completed. Mom hated going because she felt they should be doing more advanced treatments for her so she could get back to swimming. I just let her fuss as I opened up a container of turkey bacon, which I fried up before leaving the house. Mom's appetite was still a bit off, as she only ate a few bites.

She did want some coffee, so I went downstairs to the café and brought up some for both her and Mildred.

Soon, Nurse Mary walked in from the Radiology Center to explain Mom's treatment for this week. Her first appointment was scheduled for Thursday. During that treatment, they would map out the area on her hip that needed the treatment. Mom was scheduled for ten treatments that would begin the end of the week, with each treatment lasting fifteen minutes. We would meet Dr. Trenkner, the one performing the treatment, this Thursday. Mom was quiet and sullen during the nurse's visit. She offered no questions, but just stared at the TV.

Mildred left after a while, and I then offered Mom another massage with her favorite eucalyptus and peppermint oil. She really enjoyed the feel of the oils and the smells. She and I both were growing weary of the hospital smells and the inability for her to take a real bath. Still, as luck would have it, the nurse came in again and told Mom she would be getting a real bath tomorrow. They would even wash her hair as well.

That brought a smile to her face that quickly went away as the aide came by to take her to therapy again. This time, the aide made her walk down to the gym using her walker – oh my goodness! Mom fussed at the aide the entire walk down the hall! When she came back to the room, she looked extremely tired and fought taking a nap like a four-year-old. I hung out with her until about 4:00 p.m., after we had watched Dr. Phil. I watered a plant that a friend had left for her and kissed her goodnight. Mom was really tired and could barely keep her eyes open.

9

DOING MORE HARM THAN GOOD?

January 25th through January 27th, 2005

I beat Mom to the punch and called her before she called me early Tuesday morning. Mom told me to take my time coming to visit, as they had her scheduled for a 9:00 a.m. session on bathing herself, and then she was off to physical therapy at 10:00. After that, they had her scheduled for an 11:00 a.m. bone scan to see if the tumors were anywhere else in her system and then, after lunch, she was to go for more physical therapy. I told her I would be by around noon. In the meantime, I would dig out Mom's car and wait to hear from Dr. Carr.

Digging out Mom's car was such a royal pain. God...How I missed snow-less California! Nevertheless, after about an hour, the job was done and the weather grew sunny and warmer. I then decided to be proactive and called Dr. Carr – foolish of me to think he would actually call me back. I did reach him and asked the tougher questions, like to what extent Mom's liver and lungs had been damaged. He really didn't give a percentage, as he could not recall from the CAT scan, but he did stress that the mass was quite large. Mom's liver was still functional, but surgery would not work for her situation. It was the same thing with her lungs. Damn!

Concerning the bone marrow test, I told him she had an appointment with him for February 1st. I asked him the actual purpose of the bone marrow test, since he already determined by way of the other scans that she had large tumors in three areas of her body. Dr. Carr cited that the test could give him a better sense of how progressed the cancer was, and to offer a better prognosis. However, the procedure could possibly damage or cause her other hip to crack, thus hampering her ability to walk. I told him I objected to putting my mother through more unnecessary pain, especially if it would not serve any real purpose.

Dr. Carr citied he did not think Mom would go for the chemo and agreed the test should be postponed until we saw how she did with the radiation of the tumor in her hip. He felt and understood my concern for my mother and said he did not want to cause her more pain either. The fact was that my mother definitely had lymphoma, and the marrow test would only show us a worse picture than a better one. I told him I didn't think either Mom or myself needed to go through that. I thanked Dr. Carr for his time and ended my call.

My shaking began again ...that "unable to control shit" kind of shaking. I fumbled to call Linda for some sort of validation of what I should do, even though I already knew what to do. Linda agreed that a bone marrow test could weaken an already weak part of her body and might prove more harmful than good. She agreed with my decision to forgo it, for now.

When I hung up, I could hardly breathe. *"Am I doing what's right for Mom?"* I kept asking myself. I called Seveda, my friend in New York who had been through this same thing with her mother years earlier, for more validation. She had made some inquiries with the physicians that worked with her mother to get me the "real deal" on what my mom was facing. Seveda reported that her medical experts explained that my Mom is in the worst possible stage of lymphoma, and at this point, there was *nothing* anyone could do but to make her as comfortable as possible.

The chemo would help save her liver and lungs from failing, but it was just a matter of time. These were hard words to hear...I couldn't speak...I couldn't breathe...I hung up on my friend as I sobbed uncontrollably yet again in my mother's house...alone, by myself...but shit, this ain't about me. So how come I feel it is? This is just too much to bear!

I left the house and started shoveling snow. I shoveled snow off the porch, around other cars, off the sidewalks of neighbors, anything to keep busy and work out this overwhelming tension. I was making such a mess, my heart was about to fly out of my chest, and my tears blurred my vision. I finally sat down inside Mom's van and looked at the religious tapes strewn on top of her dash and in her glove box.

The one sticking out of her tape player was about Jesus' healing powers. I sobbed and prayed for this Jesus to heal my Mommy.

I sat in her van for what seemed forever. Finally, I pulled it together and made it to the hospital by noon. The nurse told me Mom was out having a bone scan. Mom got back to her room around 1:00 and we were told that we should get the test results back the following day.

The rest of our visit went well. I didn't tell her of my conversation with Dr. Carr – I know I would have lost it again. Mom seemed pretty tired, as she'd had a full day already. So, we kept it light and watched TV together. I left around 4:00 to visit Aunt Mable so that she and Mom could speak to each other on my cell phone. They laughed and fussed and chatted away with each other for about an hour. It was great to end the day this way.

The next morning I got up super early and went into my usual task mode. First stop: to get Mom's car to the AAA office for the new auto insurance inspection. Check. Then I went to Mom's mechanic, as Mom's passenger door and window had been acting up. I told them Mom was in the hospital and that I wanted to get it fixed before she came home. They were real nice people who were able to fix it the same day for under $300.00. Check. They even picked me up and brought me back when it was fixed. Small town hospitality – how nice.

Mom had called while I was out running around, but when I called the hospital, she was not in her room. I tried again a bit later and the nurse said she had been in therapy and was now out having an x-ray of her left shoulder. Apparently, the doctors had "found something" in the bone scan yesterday and wanted a closer look. Mom got back to her room while I was on with the nurse, so she put her on the phone.

Mom sounded super tired, and told me she had had three more PT sessions. I tried to distract her with tales of my adventures today with her car. She got upset that I spent money on her again. I told her it was something Gregor and I wanted to do and to not worry about it. I reminded her she would need her car to work when she gets home. That was something she could not argue with.

I then reminded Mom that she has her first appointment at the radiation center the following day. Mom had totally forgotten about it. I told her I would be with her tomorrow, but needed to be at the house today to wait for Sears to come by to fix the washer. Mom almost argued with me again, but knew it would be futile. I instead asked if she had eaten her breakfast and lunch, and she reported she was only able to get down half of both.

The Sears tech came on time to look at the washing machine. He said it only needed a five-dollar pipe and then proceeded to cancel the work order so I did not have to pay him the $55 service call – again, wonderful Hoosier, home-town hospitality! How nice! I then went to Lowe's, found the pipe he spoke of, and fixed the bloody washing machine myself!

I called Mom later in the day. She sounded tired after her very exhausting day. Still, she got to play bingo as part of her therapy. They placed weights on her arms to exercise them, and she had won a tee shirt! She actually sounded happy over that – she loves tee shirts. Mom even changed her clothes and wore her own sweats and tee shirt today. She wants me to bring in a laundry bag to collect her dirties. I told her the washing machine was fixed, so clean clothes should not be a problem.

The next morning, I got an early start and arrived at the hospital around 8:30 a.m. Mom was up and dressed, and while she was lying down on the bed, she looked good and forced a smile my way. I could sense her nervousness over the first radiation treatment. Nurse Debra had shared with me that Mom had only eaten half of her breakfast. The nurse inspects Mom's tray after each meal, much to Mom's displeasure, so Mom's been finding ways to trick them. She clearly has no appetite and will only eat a few bites of each meal. She has been enjoying her butter-pecan Ensure drink, but today she has two of them left on the table beside her bed.

Mom really did look great this morning. She happily shared that she had been able to take another shower today and washed her hair with her favorite shampoo that I had brought several days ago. Nurse Debra told us that Mom was scheduled to remain in the hospital throughout her radiation treatments, and that after that, it would be up to her depending on what she decided what to do concerning the chemo.

I questioned if it was necessary for her to undergo the bone marrow test, since her condition had already been determined. I mean, why put her through that pain and risk breaking the other hip? Nurse Debra agreed with me and said Mom and I should speak more with Dr. Carr. Mom remained mute throughout our conversation. She just looked at the TV while we talked.

I then asked the nurse about the bone scan test results. Nurse Debra said Dr. Trenkner would be going over all of that with us today, but she did disclose that the scan had found a small spot on the L5, the lumbar portion of her spine – same with her left shoulder, in addition to a bone spur in her arm. She cautioned that these may just be spots of arthritis, but the doctor would provide more details this afternoon.

Soon, staff arrived to take Mom to her daily physical therapy session. The van to the radiation center would come for her around 12:30 p.m., so it looks like another busy day for Mom. She came back from PT looking tired and frustrated, but she seemed eager to head outside, even if just for a van ride.

Nurse Debra and Mary from the radiation center cautioned that Mom should take her pain pills prior to leaving because the procedure was going to be "somewhat uncomfortable". What the hell did that mean? When I questioned them, they indicated that she'd be lying on a hard table for the fifteen-minute session. Mom took her pills and shortly after, the van staff came to get us. I got to ride with Mom in the van.

Dr. Trenkner was waiting for us at the center and went over what would be done today. They would first map out the area on her hip, and that would take about twenty minutes. Dr. Carr wanted her to begin treatment ASAP, so she would begin her first session today. She has a team of three technicians - Terry, Laura, and Shelly, who would tend to her every day. It appeared to me that they had scheduled her for afternoon treatments at around 2:00ish. Each Friday, following each session, they would draw blood to check on her progress. Every Monday, Dr. Trenkner would meet with her to review her progress.

It was a long day at the center. Mom grew impatient and began fussing about how doctors don't know what's really going on inside of her, and that her pain could all just be arthritis. I just let her fuss. After it was over, she said she would not go through this again. I knew she was just fussing again, but part of me worried that I was permitting them to do more harm than good to my mother.

Damn, she had Stage Four cancer, and nothing could be done...those words kept spinning through my head as I looked at my exhausted mother. Am I doing right by her?

When we finally got back to the hospital, Mom was pooped. Her dinner came, but she did not eat any of it. I got a salad and picked up some chicken tenders for her – one of which she ate. We watched the last half hour of Oprah, and then I could see she needed to take a nap. I tucked her in and kissed her goodbye.

10

A BITCHY FEW DAYS

Friday January 28th through January 30th, 2005

Mom called at 8:00 a.m. I was half-sleep, but faked being awake, as usual. She wanted to remind me to bring her some bras. At first, she had not wanted any since she'd lost so much weight, especially in her breasts. However, now she wanted them, even if they were too big. She said they had her scheduled for four therapy sessions today, all to take place before her early afternoon radiation treatment. I told her I would be in by 11:00.

After showering, I gathered the bras and headed to the nursing home to visit Aunt Mable. For some reason, I was feeling a bit bitchy about her living circumstances at the nursing home, so I had made it a point to meet with the administration to determine when Aunt Mable would be moved back into her regular room, where she'd have access to a phone.

I met with Janet, the program administrator, and indicated that Aunt Mable was currently living with a roommate who was comatose most of the time, and how that scenario was not appropriate for my aunt, who liked communicating with people. Auntie also had no phone in her room, like she used to, and we were now unable to call her frequently, as we did in the past.

I explained that my mother was hospitalized with a broken hip (I shared no more than that) and that Aunt Mable was aware of this. Also, I told her that my mother had explained to me that Aunt Mable had been temporarily moved from her previous room due to maintenance and painting.

Janet explained that Aunt Mable had been moved due to the renovations, but they were now reserving that wing of rooms for their short-term patients. Her current room was permanent, but they were aware of and realized her roommate situation was less than desirable due to the roommate's lack of activity.

Regarding the phone, they planned to place phones in each room as they continued their renovations, but that would take time. She promised that the nurse would make sure that any calls that come in for my aunt would be brought to her via their cordless office phone. However, as far as a more talkative roommate, Janet claimed they were waiting on permission from us to say it was okay to move Aunt Mable again. Neither Mom nor I had been informed of this, but I gave the okay to move her into a room with someone more compatible with her personality.

Following my visit with the administrator, I made my way down the hall to visit with Auntie. I found her in the dining area, nibbling on a muffin and sipping coffee. I hugged and kissed her, and then sat with her for a while. Before leaving, Janet approached me and indicated they would be having a team meeting today, where they would bring up the subject of moving my aunt. I gave her my cell and home numbers so she could reach me regarding the progress and resolution of their meetings.

Aunt Mable looked so sweet. It breaks my heart to see her here. She's so innocent in all of this, but she says they keep her busy. She asked about Mom and I told her she was doing better – which was true, to a point. She gave me the biggest hug, like she did not want to let me go. It just broke my heart.

I made it to the hospital by 11:30. I picked up some KFC along the way and got some wings for Mom. She was in a seriously fussy mood when I walked into her room. She fussed about them waking her up early for breakfast, fussed about the four physical therapy sessions for today, fussed about them fussing about her not eating. She was just plain bitchy! Mom swore up and down she was not going to take any more of their, *"stupid iron pills,"* because, *"I've not had a bowel movement in three days!"* Mom complained that the nurse had given her a suppository the previous evening but it did no good.

Needless to say, Mom was in a foul mood *all* day. Lunch came and, of course, she refused to eat it and she didn't eat the wings I brought either. She bitched and fussed with her roommate, Mary, and said she was going to throw out this meal like she did last night's meal. UGH! Still feeling a bit bitchy myself, I interjected, *"Well, if you want to go home, you better eat!"* Lawd, have mercy, why did I say that?

"I can go home anytime if I wasn't in so much pain!" Mom exclaimed.

I sat quietly for a moment and then got up, retrieved my phone and my purse, and said I would be right back. I walked over to the elevators and called Linda. Linda let me vent and we laughed it off. I know Mom feels helpless, I know she feels out of control, and this illness is making her feel crazy. I just wish there was something more I could do.

I took a deep breath, went to get a soda (or "pop" as they call it in Indiana), grabbed some low-carb cookies and then ventured back into the Queen Bee's lion's den. Fortunately, I ran into an old neighborhood friend in the cafeteria and had something new to talk about with Mom when I got back upstairs.

The therapists soon came to get her for her last physical therapy session before going to radiation. I waited in the room, relishing the silence. Not long afterward, Mom came back tired and laid down before we headed out in the Ambulette. Ray and Lee were on time picking us up, and Mom began joking around with them. Who the hell was this person? Just this morning, she had been ready to burn Parkview Hospital down!

Mom's always been fond of young men. Not in a sexual way, but in a flirtatious, playful way, if that makes sense. Anyway, she sure liked joking with Ray and Lee. Again, she fussed all the way to the center, citing that they had taken too long yesterday and they better not take as long today.

We arrived to her appointment about five minutes early and they got her in within minutes. We were out of there before 2:30. *Thank God!*

Mom liked being outside. The cool air on her face, even if it was so briefly while being placed in the Ambulette, made her feel better. The folks at the center had been nice and now she was on her way back to her room at the hospital without too much fussing.

I, on the other hand, started feeling achy on the ride back, and even more so once we got back in the room. *Damn*, my period was starting – no wonder I'd been so bitchy today! I hung out for a while and left a half hour into the Dr. Phil show. Mom was tired too. Despite the madness of the day, I kissed Mommy goodnight and gave her a big hug.

The next morning, Mom called early, as usual, to tell me that she was scheduled to have PT, even on a Saturday! I told her I would be there by noon. She also asked me to bring some of the Carol Burnett Show VHS tapes I bought for her last year. My period was in full-gush stream and cramps had raised their ugly head. Still, I felt glad that I had a few hours to just chill.

I made it to the hospital by 10:30 but when I got there, Mom was in therapy. A male therapist brought her back to the room by 11:30. She was in a pretty good mood and joking with him. I loaded up the Carol Burnett videos and we shared some laughs. My favorite nurse, Debra, was there, and she told me that Mom's staples would be coming out on Monday after her radiation. I also asked when she might be going home, and she told us it looked like the week of February 7th.

Mom and I hung out for a while, watching the videos until Linda called. Her daughter was in town from college and Linda wondered if I wanted to join them for lunch. Mom was getting sleepy, so I left around 2:30 and met up with them. It was a good diversion from my usual routine, but no sooner had we made it halfway through our meal, it started snowing *again*. I had wanted to get rid of my rental car since it looked like I would be in Fort Wayne for a while, and Mom had a perfectly good car for me to use. We quickly finished our meals and they followed me to the airport so I could return my rental car. They took me back to Mom's house, where I got Mom's van. Damn, the snow was really starting to come down. Later that evening, I called Mom and checked in on her. She sounded fine, and had just finished visiting with Cousin Mildred.

Watching the snow fall and accumulate was becoming too commonplace in Fort Wayne, at least as far as I was concerned. By Sunday morning, we ended up getting about five more inches of snow, and driving Mom's van was a royal pain in the ass; it's bigger than any car I've driven in a while. It's like driving a large anteater – the snout on this van is long and ugly.

Mom called bright and early the next morning and said it was okay if I didn't come visit, due to the snow. I had laundry to do and some house cleaning, plus I needed to do grocery shopping. Surprisingly, even with all that running around, I did manage to get by the hospital about mid-afternoon. I brought Mom two more Carol Burnett videos, some clean clothes, and picked up two personal pan pizzas from Pizza Hut for us to munch on. The Sunday meals at the hospital are usually pretty lame.

Mom looked good and was proud to proclaim that she made herself have a bowel movement. The way she did it, however, is not something I would recommend - using a gloved hand up her ass to "*grab the turd.*" Mom always loved to be overly graphic with her description of anything gross! She said she had three bowel movements after digging around in her ass. She clearly has no personal filters when it comes to expressing herself.

We spent the afternoon watching the Carol Burnett videos. Linda stopped by to visit around 4:00 and that pleased me. Mom enjoyed Linda's company and they had a good visit. We talked for about an hour before Linda and I left Mom to eat her dinner. We gave her a big kiss goodbye and wished her sweet dreams.

I was restless after visiting Mom, so I drove the anteatermobile around the south side of Ft. Wayne, as I wasn't ready to go home. I actually saw the sun set over what used to be Southtown Mall. Sadly, the mall was now just an empty large lot that looks out on several closed stores and a new Big K. I parked and debated about going inside, but I wasn't feeling it. I decided instead to go up to Scott's Market for some groceries and detergent.

As I drove, I felt extremely lonely and tired. I really missed Gregor and our dog, Zorro. I felt like cooking, but had no one to cook for. As I made my way into Scott's, I walked around aimlessly for a while. I suddenly broke into tears after I heard a squeaky toy going off a few aisles over. The sound made me think of my silly dog. Damn! I really missed home.

Dammit Nat, stop it, I scolded myself. I have got to pull it together. Later, back home, I tried calling Gregor, but the phone just rang and rang. I then tried calling Tonya to see if she wanted to get together – no answer there either. Damn. I hate this feeling. I have got to focus on something else other than my feelings. My colleague, Dr. Pat, from my former job in New York City, called this morning to see how I was doing. I offered a strong front, but I really hate trying to be strong for my friends and I hate falling apart with my friends. I do wish I could pull it together.

11

COUNTDOWN TO RADIATION AND MORE BAD NEWS

Monday January 31st through February 1st, 2005

I'm so incredibly tired this morning - I just couldn't fall asleep last night. I had the TV on until 3:00 a.m. and Mom called at her usual 8:00 time. I felt so groggy I couldn't even fake it for her. She has therapy twice this morning, so she told me to take my time coming over. That worked out well since I was so tired. I needed to make a run to Dr. Carr's office to get the update on those other questions I had, and I needed to make a run to Aunt Mable's to make sure they were doing what I needed them to do for her move to a new room.

When I arrived at Dr. Carr's facility, he was not in. His nurse, Margaret, was at Parkview, so the receptionist paged her for me. I waited a while and was able to cancel Mom's bone marrow appointment for the following day, and then left to try to catch the nurse at the hospital. As soon as I got to the car, my cell phone rang – it was Tonya. I debated about answering and decided I needed to tell her what was up. She was dealing with drama from one of her children at the laundromat just down the street. I told her that I was close to the laundromat, and decided to go over there and meet her and tell her everything.

I pulled into the parking lot and saw Tonya flagging me down as I maneuvered the anteater-mobile. Once inside the building, she expressed her concern over my fatigue. I brushed that off and asked her to sit down. I began by telling her she was not to disclose any of what I was about to tell her to *anyone* – not her mother, her children, *no one*! I told her Mom and I do not want this broadcast on the Ft. Wayne gossip line, and she agreed. Actually, she suspected the bad news I was about to tell her – I could see it in her eyes. I cried like a baby as I told her, and she was surprisingly strong and supportive.

While we talked, my cell rang; I saw that it was Nurse Margaret and took the call. She and Dr. Aggarwal, from Dr. Carr's group, were speaking with Mom and the doctor wanted to speak with me as well. The doctor got on the phone and was very direct with her information. As a colleague of Dr. Carr's, she had just gone over "things" with Mom. She was in agreement with me that a bone marrow test at this point would serve no purpose. She had examined Mom and noticed that she felt a possible new mass in her pancreas.

Dr. Aggarwal confirmed that Mom appeared to have Stage Four lymphoma, and that the best course of treatment would be the IV type of chemotherapy. However, Mom's prognosis of survival with this aggressively spreading cancer could be less than one-month survival rate if she did nothing, and perhaps six to twelve months if she underwent aggressive chemo.

Mom could not begin the chemo while she was undergoing the radiation treatment, due to severe toxicological side effects. In addition, the side effects of the extra medication could potentially cause Mom to have a heart attack – something neither of us wanted. The doctor said my mother was not "feeling" what she said and wanted me to talk to her about the pros and cons of the treatment.

I drank in everything the doctor said and then called Linda. I ended up leaving a message for her with the latest news, and just stood in front of the laundromat, feeling numb. I turned to look at my best friend and she knew, without me saying a word. I again blubbered like an idiot for what seemed like forever. However, I eventually pulled myself together, as I soon had to take off for the hospital. Tonya made me promise to call her later.

During my drive to Parkview, my head raced, absorbing the recent information, trying my best not to break down again. When I arrived at the hospital, Mom was eating lunch. The moment she saw me, she immediately began to fuss about Dr. Aggarwal. Mom made some awful racist comment about her being an Indian (from India) and complained that she was using scare tactics to make her use chemo. Nothing I said would calm her down at this point, as she was totally against any type of chemo. So, I just let her rant and rave.

After a few minutes, Mom stared at me and I started to cry. I told her that I loved her too much to not do my best to fight for her life. Mom continued to stare at me, but said nothing. She chilled out as we both changed the subject. Television served as a great diversion for Mom; she started flipping through channels and turned to "Judge TV," which we watched in silence until the nurse came and told us it was time to remove Mom's hip staples. I so wanted to leave the room, but Mom asked me to stay. So, I turned my squeamish head in the opposite direction and thought of being in sunny California. The nurse was gentle and Mom seemed to feel better once they were removed.

Soon after that, Lee and Joe came to take us to radiation therapy. We met with Dr. Trenkner afterwards, who had better luck and did a better job at easing Mom's mind about what chemo was all about and how her survival rates would be reduced if she did nothing. Mom wanted a promise that if she did the chemo, the cancer would go away. Of course, he could not promise that since her cancer was so advanced, but on a positive note, he did indicate that Mom's blood count was up. Shit, finally some good news!

Mom did pretty well with her treatment and got a kick out of bantering with Lee and Joe. We made it back to the room, where it felt a bit chilly. Mom wanted to curl up under her covers and relax. She received a phone call, so while she was on the phone, I stepped out and called Linda and Gregor with the new information. Both were upset that more cancer has been found in her pancreas. I told Linda that I had not been able to reach Cousin Shirley, but would try again tonight.

Mom and I then watched some more TV and I left later that afternoon to go to Kinko's to pick up a fax from Gregor regarding Project Renew, a housing improvement program Mom wanted to explore to fix her and Aunt Mable's house.

Tonya called on my drive out to Kinko's to tell me she was on her way to visit my Mom with her daughters. She promised not to bring up our conversation about Mom's illness. Later that evening, Tonya called to tell me that Mom actually disclosed her health issues and brought up the subject of chemotherapy. She even brought up the fact that everyone wanted her to do it, and how I got so emotional. Wow…that's surprising. Mom rarely shares her business like that, but it was good to hear she opened up to Tonya.

Later that evening, I finally got in touch and spoke at length with my Cousin Shirley. Shirley's Dad, who had since passed away, and my Dad were brothers. We always got along and I often enjoyed visiting with her whenever I made it back to Fort Wayne. She has a cool, calm, mellow sense about her that I admired and respected. She never judged me, and she always kept me in the family loop. I informed her about what was going on with Mom, as they had always shared a close and loving relationship.

I asked Shirley for assistance in looking out for Mom once I returned to California. She offered to do whatever she could, since she was not presently working. I told her that I would pay her – which she declined – but I will do so anyway. She discussed the pros and cons of making Mom go through such intensive chemo treatments, especially in light of how it would exhaust her and prevent her from leading an active life like she'd been used to. Considering Mom's age and how far advanced this cancer was, Shirley said I needed to think about what Mom wanted most – to maintain her dignity, mobility, and independence.

Strangely, when I spoke with Gregor later, he too said I should consider treating her holistically, because at her age, chemo could cause more harm than good. Damn, *am I* doing more harm than good? Am I being selfish to keep my mother with me longer regardless of how it affected her? Shit, I needed to pray on this.

The next morning arrived, but I felt incredibly tired. I had been up until 3:00 a.m., praying through the night about this chemo madness. I still didn't have any answers. For some reason, Mom didn't call this morning like she normally did. I didn't sense anything was wrong, so I decided to go by the nursing home and visit Aunt Mable before checking in on Mom.

When I arrived at the nursing home, I found Auntie sitting out in the front lobby with the other residents in a semi-circle. They were preparing for a church service – communion and all. I hugged and kissed Auntie and told her I would be back after speaking with the social worker, who was in her office.

Janet apologized for not getting back with me. She claimed that she had "lost my numbers". . *Are you fuckin' kidding me?* I thought. Still, one cannot be shitty to someone who is charged with caring for your Auntie, right? So, I just bit my tongue and repeated my numbers while she noted them in her Rolodex.

Concerning the move for my aunt, she indicated that as per our last meeting, she wanted to try to connect her with a woman who appeared sweet, but had been in an odd mood this past week, which would not make for a great match with my Auntie. They had run some medical tests on the proposed roommate to see what was going on, and would have the results by Thursday. They didn't want to upset both women by disrupting their routines if the proposed match would not work out. Fine. Janet would have until Monday to do something about this, or I will begin to lose my patience.

By the time I got back out front, Auntie was singing with the others. I didn't want to disturb her or the service, so I left. I told a staff member to tell her I would swing by later in the week. Aunt Mable's Seventh-day Adventist church family has been a Godsend. They came by every single day and communicated with me at least three times a week to let me know they had been out to see her. They've even taken her off-site to their church for Saturday services. I've never seen a congregation so dedicated to caring for one of their members as much as they care for my Auntie Mable.

Since it was still early, I made it over to the health food store next to my old high school to look up books on alternative methods to deal with cancer. They had tons of literature there, along with food, vitamins, and helpful staff who assisted me in finding the appropriate herbs for Mom. I picked up several items that were mentioned in a couple of books for Mom to read, think about, and hopefully, use.

I finally made it to the hospital just before noon. Mom sat on the edge of the bed, having just returned from her third physical therapy session. She was tired, but in good spirits. I told her I had gone to the health food store and brought some alternative treatment literature. I confessed that just like the way she felt about imposing her feelings against nursing homes for Aunt Mable, perhaps I was imposing my feelings about her taking chemo. I told Mom that if she didn't want to go through that madness, then I should listen to what she wanted and not focus only on what I wanted.

I explained that I had a long talk with Cousin Shirley, who has gone through this chemo thing with a dear friend. The side effects were not pretty. I told Mom I wanted her to have the best quality of life possible and who knows? Trying herbal methods may work for her. I then showed her the herbal pills I had picked up, and the books. Mom didn't say much, but began to read one of the books and appeared to really get into it. She looked over the herbal pills and opened them up. Mom said she thinks she can give it a good fight just as long as she's not burning out her insides. At last... something we both agreed on.

I also brought Mom her bills and she went at them as if she were sitting in her living room at home. While we worked on the bills, in walked Dr. Carr's nurse, Margaret, the day nurse, Debra, and Dr. Aggarwal. They seemed to be pleased, thinking I was there to help convince Mom to go for the chemo treatment. Funny, they had no idea that we just agreed to *not* to go the chemotherapy route. However, I was friendly and polite as we re-introduced ourselves. Mom looked up at them, said nothing, and scowled at Dr. Aggarwal.

I did ask Margaret about what type of diet mom would have to adhere to while on chemo, but there was no special diet required. As far as length of treatment, Margaret said that Mom would go for one day every three weeks. The first day would be the worst and the longest, taking eight to nine hours. That session was longer because the body might have an adverse reaction to the drugs if infused too quickly. They would send her home with a prescription to take for five days after the first treatment. The subsequent treatments would last four to five hours. When asked if Mom could drive herself to treatment, they told her "no," as they would be giving her meds that would cause drowsiness.

Mom listened and kept shaking her head while she focused on her bills. Debra kept asking Mom if she was listening, and I could see Mom was getting pissed at the questioning and staring. I politely shooed them away and asked if they could put in writing the medications Mom would be taking so we could absorb it all. The doctor left abruptly; she seemed upset with Mom's lack of "respect" toward the situation. Little did they know that both of us had already made up our minds against their treatment plan.

Lee and Joe arrived on time to take Mom to radiation, which didn't last long. Despite the visit with the doctor earlier in the morning, it was a good day - one we've not had in a while. The nurse came after we returned from radiation treatment to take Mom for her evening bath, something she really looked forward to, so I left. I pray that I'm helping Mom make the right decision.

I was seriously craving some carbs, so I ended up going to the local BBQ joint and got some short ribs, mac and cheese, and greens. I later called Linda and Gregor and told them about the day. Linda said she had called Gordon and left a message on his voicemail, fussing him out for not calling and checking in on Mom. He did call my voicemail later and left a message - more like a crappy excuse - as to why he's not called...whatever. I would not be calling him back; he needed to come and see *his* mother.

Before I ate, I called Seveda. I needed to know if there was ever a time throughout her ordeal with her mother's illness that she felt she did not do the right thing, or not enough? She said that toward the end, when the doctors suggested they do things that would do nothing to extend her life, or quality of life, she had to put her foot down and say "no more". Seveda understands that although we as children want our parents to live forever, there comes a time when we have to trust in what *they* want for their life.

Mom is totally aware of who she is and where she is. She is lucid about what's going on around her. Just because she refuses to *accept* what the doctors predict for her does not make her crazy. I mean, what if she is right? She's been pretty healthy for seventy-three years. It's true that doctors told her she could not and should not get pregnant again after her ectopic pregnancy with Gordon... But damn, here I am; living proof of her refusal to believe in what *"they"* said. Perhaps her tenacity and faith will carry her through this madness. I'd rather have whatever time she has left spent hugging me, and not the toilet!

12

THE KINDNESS OF STRANGERS – AND ANOTHER FRUSTRATING WEEK

February 2ⁿᵈ through February 6ᵗʰ, 2005

I have been dealing with insomnia, but last night, I finally fell asleep around midnight. Unfortunately, I had a horrible dream and woke up at 6:00 a.m. I tried to fall back to sleep, without success. It didn't help that Mom called about an hour later, asking me to bring some type of a thinner headband for her hair. She keeps having these insane night sweats – from the cancer?

After her call, I got up, showered, and then took the bills to the post office and ran the cable bill out to Comcast. I then headed to Big K to get the headbands. Hell, I got one for me too! By the time I arrived at the hospital, she was in physical therapy, according to her roommate, Mary. I went downstairs and got us coffee to go with the breakfast I had picked up at Burger King.

Mom was gone about an hour before she came back to the room. She said she had a great night's sleep without any pain, even without a pain pill last night. Wow, that was great news. She would have two more therapy sessions today, and they had re-scheduled her radiation for later as they wanted to take an x-ray of her leg. What's that about?

Mom ate a few bites of the breakfast sandwich and drank half the coffee. I was pleased to see her eat. Mom said she had also eaten the hospital breakfast – one boiled egg, one piece of bacon, and one slice of toast. Nice job, Mom! Perhaps a better appetite meant she was getting better? One can only hope.

They soon brought lunch, but Mom was not hungry. Apparently, Mom has not pooped since her little "digging" expedition four days ago. We shared this with Nurse Debra and Dr. Wallace, who stopped in on Mom during my visit. Dr. Wallace said he would get Mom some "liquid dynamite" to relieve her constipation after she returned from radiation.

I brought Mom the rest of the bills that Aunt Mable pays and we worked on those. She seemed really happy doing the bills – being in control really means a lot to her. Mom said she'd been taking the herbal medicine I brought yesterday and took some with her breakfast. She re-affirmed that she believes this will work for her, and in no way does she want chemo.

Joe came late, without Lee, for our trip to radiation. Because we went later in the day, we stayed longer, after which they took the additional x-rays. The visit seemed to last *forever* today. I think I read through everything I had brought with me and even edited the photos on my cell phone. I was so tired and soon began to grow anxious, as the technician's kept coming out reassuring me that Mom was, *"Doing fine and would be out soon."*

How I wished they would just be quiet, because they were stressing me out. Shit, I began to hyperventilate and had to go outside to call Gregor. I told him I didn't know why I was having this panic attack, but it was messing with my head. Joe came to get me a few minutes later and we all left to return to the hospital. On the way, I wondered what the hell was that panic attack about?

Back in Mom's room, the nurse brought in the "liquid thunder" tonic, aka citrus nitrate, which Mom hated. I reminded her that she was the one who complained about not being able to have a bowel movement for days, and this was guaranteed to work.

Tonya soon called and said she was on her way over with a ton of Girl Scout cookies that Mom had ordered weeks ago. Tonya and her daughters arrived, and for some reason they all were quite exhausting to be around. Perhaps I was just overtired from the past few days, and I'd not eaten since this morning. I don't know, but I just wanted to sit and chill, but felt unable to. While Mom was glad to see them, I was glad they left after an hour. Mom had yet to poop, although she had taken the entire bottle of citrus nitrate. I hoped she would relieve herself before she went to sleep.

On my way home, I stopped by T-Mobile to get a "pay-as-you-go" cell phone for Cousin Shirley so she could call me long distance after I left. It also has voice mail, so I could leave her a message. This should work out with her looking in on Mom.

The next morning, Mom called bright and early as usual. She told me she needed more underwear as the citrus nitrate worked right after I had left last night. She'd made it to the bathroom without any mishaps the first four times, but through the night she thought she only had gas – but was wrong and messed her undies a little bit. She laughed about how much that "liquid dynamite" worked and vowed never to take it again. She tried to eat her cereal that morning, but it caused another gastric eruption. I told her I would bring more undies.

On my way to the hospital, I paid a visit to "Project Renew", a neighborhood revitalization program Mom and I had signed up for last August. We wanted to fix up her house and the house next door, (Aunt Mable's former house), so Gregor and I could have a place to stay when we visited them. Aunt Mable had given me her place years earlier, and I always thought it would be cool to connect the two in some way.

I was at Project Renew to drop off my application paperwork to a woman named Ramona. We went over my application and changed some of the things I wanted done to the house. I explained that I would be going back to California soon, and she promised to get back with me with the final amount of the new rehab loan before I left town. I didn't share Mom's situation with her, as I didn't feel it was necessary at this point.

After that visit, I drove to Big K to purchase another package of underwear, and then to Taco Bell to get some tacos for Mom. When I arrived in her room, she was sitting up and watching TV. I noticed that her headband kept sliding off and that I really need to get her hair cut. Mom's reluctance to let me cut it - control issues - didn't stop her from fussing about getting her hair done.

She changed the subject and spoke instead of her continued diarrhea runs to the bathroom since last night. Mom was afraid to try the taco for fear she may have to make a mad dash to the bathroom. After some coaxing, she took a few bites, as she could not resist the aroma. Just as she anticipated, she had to go to the bathroom a few minutes later, but she made it in time. We then watched television while I straightened the room, gathering her dirties to take home to do laundry.

When lunch came, Mom only ate the Jell-O. The grilled cheese looked "tight" so she ate more of her taco. After lunch, the therapists came to get her for her last physical therapy session, after which Lee came to take us to radiation. While I waited for Mom, I called a friend in New York and she said a prayer for us. The treatment went quickly. Fortunately, I didn't have another panic attack.

Back at the hospital, we watched some more TV until Mom dozed off. I soon left to go visit Aunt Mable at the nursing home and to check in with the social worker about her room change.

Wow, it was noticeably warmer outside today, so the drive to the nursing home was nice. Aunt Mable was in her room watching Judge Joe Brown. She looked good and asked how Mom was. I told her she would be coming home next week, and Auntie was really glad. I called Mom from my cell phone so she and Aunt Mable could talk. They sounded so cute talking to each other, each one telling the other: *"You better listen to your doctor!"* They really do love each other and I could see Aunt Mable was worried about Mom. I hung out for a while and then looked for the social worker.

I found Janet, the social worker out front with one of the maintenance workers. I asked about the status of moving Aunt Mable and she said they were still working on it. Their testing of a possible roommate "Clyde", (a female), showed nothing physically wrong, but they still could not ascertain why she'd suddenly become so crabby. They are still looking to move the two of them into a room together, but now they were waiting on a room.

Janet began to walk me down the hall where they wanted to put the two. There, the maintenance worker indicated that, perhaps, they could put them in Room 109, as it was newly painted and only holding furniture for now. He opened the door for us to expose a nice big room. Janet thought it would be good for them and would have Aunt Mable look at the room tomorrow to see if she wanted the window bed or the door bed. *Finally!* I thanked Janet and told her Mom would be leaving the hospital next week.

That night, I took some knockoff version of Nyquil and fell asleep *fast.* I woke up at 8:30 the next morning, surprised that Mom had not called. I called her and learned she had had a rough night. She hadn't taken her pain pill. For some reason, she feels she doesn't need to take anything, but the down side is that she woke up in pain - so much so that she grew nauseous.

Mom said she would be leaving for physical therapy soon. I told her I would pick up some chicken (her favorite) and would make it there by 11:00. I arrived with the chicken, along with her laundry and a new bra I had picked up at Target. I also brought her clippers and scissors to cut her hair.

As I approached Mom's room, I saw a woman doing the hair of another patient two rooms down. I dropped off my stuff in Mom's room and went back to speak with the lady about cutting Mom's hair. As it turned out, this woman, named Gwen, works out of her home and had a moment to come by to cut Mom's hair – and she only charged $18.

Gwen was quite engaging with Mom and her roommate, Mary, who also wanted her hair cut and curled. It was fun watching them act like young girls. I was surprised that Mom actually relented and let someone else be in control of her hair. I knew she had dreaded my trying to cut it. Gwen did a very nice job cutting and curling Mom's hair. She quickly did Mary's hair as well, as she was being released today. Mary and her hubby really appreciated it. Gwen was so taken with both ladies that she refused to take any money. Instead, she requested that we donate to the Ronald McDonald wing of the hospital. I ended up sneaking twenty dollars in her smock pocket as she left the room.

Mom looked great and loved her cut/curl. She told me that she was told they would be taking her down for more x-rays today, but no one could tell her why. Mom also said she wanted to see her x-rays because she did not believe she had a broken hip. *Really*, Mom? Where was this coming from?

I walked outside Mom's room and grabbed the first nurse I saw and asked her about seeing the x-rays. She told me I would have to call Dr. Gertsen and gave me his number. I called his office and after many transfers, I was connected to

Nurse Denise. I told her what I wanted, but she dismissed my request, as Dr. Gertsen was in surgery at Parkview and would not be available until Monday.

I told her that all I needed was to look at the x-rays and the hospital had already said it was okay. Denise put it back on the nurses at Parkview and again said that Dr. Gertsen would not be available until Monday. I asked her if she could page him. She chuckled, and with a tone of sarcasm, said she could leave him a message. Are you kidding me? Why, oh why, did that heifer laugh and act so dismissive?

The "Opal Jean" in me jumped out as I quickly snapped back at her: *"So, you find this funny? You find my frustration and need for information funny? I find that very unprofessional. Now I know the doctor is not in surgery every hour of every minute of every day, so kindly page him and leave him a message to call me today!"*

Denise denied laughing and shut down after I broke on her. She said she would leave a message. I then marched down the hall and told Melissa what that cow said about Dr. Gertsen being at Parkview. I asked her to have him paged too.

About an hour later, I was in Mom's room watching her do her bedside physical therapy with Rachel when the phone rang. I picked it up and, low and behold, it was Dr. Gertsen! He kindly explained that the need for more x-rays today on Mom's hip was a follow-up and said we could look at the x-rays. He said due to "modern technology" the films were on the computer, and he would have the nurse set it up and bring it in for us to review. He also stated he would be seeing Mom in six weeks to check on the healing. I thanked him for his time and told Mom what he said. She seemed cool, but also leery that perhaps she didn't break her hip after all, and they were lying to her. I thought, *Oh, for goodness sake, Mom! Now there's a conspiracy?*

After her workout, Mom took a brief nap before Lee came to take us to her radiation therapy. Mom was in good spirits and enjoyed getting outside, even if it was just for the brief ride to the radiation center. While waiting for her, I ran into Nurse Mary, who asked how *I* was doing. Not Mom, but me. She noticed I was looking at a medical supply book and I told her I was looking to get bathroom aids for Mom for when she goes home.

She asked whether I spoken with any case managers about obtaining supplies and services for Mom since she'd been diagnosed with cancer. I told her I had not. She left and returned shortly with Lynn, a case manager, who told me about Cancer Services, an organization that offers any type of medical supplies, free, that Mom might need for her return home. They had an abundant supply of beds, shower chairs, toilet raisers, etc. She gave me their pamphlet and I called them when we got back to the hospital. Their staff explained that I would have to come in to their office to enroll Mom, which would take about thirty minutes, and they would go over all their supplies that I could take right then and there.

I told Mom about it. At first, she balked, but I convinced her it would save *me* money if her insurance would not cover it. Ever since I had returned to Ft. Wayne, Mom had constantly complained that I was spending way too much money on her and the house. Even though I fussed back at her that it was *my* money to spend, Mom was having problems accepting assistance from me. So, once I threw her words back at her, she had no choice but to receive the assistance from Cancer Services. Score *ONE* for the daughter!

I hung out with Mom until Nurse Melissa came in with the computer to look at Mom's x-rays. Mom could clearly see the vertical break in her bone, close to the hip socket. We then looked at the rod that had been inserted into the bone joining the socket. That rod was connected to a longer rod that ran the length of her left thigh bone. Since this was an x-ray, we could not see the tumor, but we were able to review the x-ray they had taken earlier today. The radiation was helping the bone heal, but it would take some time. Nurse Melissa also explained that, per orders from both Dr.'s Wallace and Gertsen, Mom can't soak in a bathtub or go swimming until her surgical wound was completely healed, as doing so, Mom could risk infection. Mom was not too pleased about this. She gets such joy out of swimming and soaking in a hot bath.

I left Mom later that afternoon to go to Cancer Services. The people there were really compassionate and professional. I met with Mom's assigned Client Advocate, Denise. She was a caring, friendly person who explained how they could help Mom and how they would keep the lines of communication open with me even after I go back to California. We went through their large inventory of supplies and they let me have a toilet booster seat and a shower chair. I took her card and thanked them for their assistance.

I was feeling lonely after all of this so, of course, I decided to find something to eat. Ahhh, comfort food, my drug of choice. I stopped by Ziffel's – a joint for ribs and chicken. Despite "rave" reviews from those who told me about this place, it really wasn't all that. Where was Brook's Ribs when you wanted some real pork? I called Gregor while I waited for my food, walking into a pet store nearby so I could pick up a toy for Zorro. Hubby was walking our pooch when I called him. I really miss my man and pup.

Saturday morning found me waking up late again. It was past 8:30 a.m., and I had not heard from Mom. When I called her, she was just drifting off for a nap. I asked her what she wanted me to bring her to eat. Mom, of course, said she had her Ensure and did not want anything. I told her I'd pick her up a sandwich and would be there shortly. She did ask me to bring her Clint Eastwood videotapes.

Since I was heading to Big K, I thought I would also try to find the video *Ray* for her. Mom's been talking about seeing it since it came out on video. Well, who knew finding a VHS tape would be like mining for gold in Indiana? Big K, Best Buy, and a local video rental store did not have it. I finally found it at Wal-Mart before I made my way into the hospital.

Mom was sitting up eating her lunch when I arrived. She actually ate half of her cheeseburger, and ate some of my fries as I ate my salad from Burger King. She looked good, but noticed that her new roommate, who is 101 years old, had a rough night. She had fallen while in a nursing home and broken her arm. She's a real sad case and Mom has taken it upon herself to look out for her with the slow nurses. That's my mother, always looking out for the underdog and taking care of others. The roommate also liked the room dark and did not turn on her TV. I asked Mom to please not sit in the dark just because her roommate hates light – it was not good for either one of them and it would lower their morale.

I pulled out the Ray video and Mom grew excited, but she was more excited when she saw the Clint Eastwood tapes. Lord, she *loves* that man. *"He's so cool,"* Mom says. Things were going pretty smooth until Dr. Wallace showed up. He asked Mom how she was, and naturally, Mom went into her spiel wondering why was it taking so long for her bone to heal and why wasn't it healed by now? She just kept fussing and complaining about the doctor's inability to "guarantee" when, how fast, and how soon she'll no longer feel pain. Oh my goodness! The doctor was patient and did his best to explain the healing process. However, Mom tuned him out as soon as she said what she wanted to say.

Soon thereafter, her friend, Mattie, from her "spa" came by to visit. I had left for a moment to call Gregor, as I really needed a break, and when I got back to her room, Mom was chatting it up with her friend. My mother so loves an audience. Any opportunity to brag how she's not going to do what the doctor's recommended, how *she* knew more than anyone else when it comes to *her* body, etc., etc.

Mom really pisses me off when she does this, because whoever she's spouting off to then looks at me to see if she's kidding, or to clarify what she's complaining about. *How I hate that!* I know Mom's scared, but she won't admit it. I know she's not used to laying around waiting for other's to tend to her. I know she feels out of control, but *damn, woman, chill out!*

I left the room briefly for some fresh air and a "pop" refill. I rejoined Mom and her company, who stayed for another twenty minutes. Mom and I hung out until about 5:00 p.m., and then left Mom with a dutiful smile on my face and a kiss on her stubborn forehead. I really need to work off this frustration. So what did I do? Went to Big K to shop again, (my other drug of choice). I picked up some cleaning supplies to continue cleaning the upper walls and the foyer of the house in preparation for Mom's return.

At the house, I washed all the towels, ran the vacuum, and changed the back door curtain. I then picked up some fried catfish from Griffin's. It was pretty good, except for the fact that they didn't include tartar sauce or hot sauce. Should I *have* to ask for such things? Regardless, it was pretty tasty, even with the bones. Don't they know the meaning of "filet"?

I called and spoke to Mom later (I was feeling kind of funky for feeling so pissed at her), but she was fine. She had visitors from Aunt Mable's church stop by, along with calls from Cousin Mildred and Tonya's mom. All in all, she'd had a pretty busy evening. She sounded tired, so I told her I loved her, and she said, *"Sweet dreams, Princess."* No matter how old I get, no matter how much we disagree, she has no idea how it touches my soul each time she calls me "Princess".

Sunday morning I slept in again and I didn't hear from Mom until around 9:00 a.m. She was up watching television and I told her I'd be by after I made a run to Lowe's. I picked up replacement handles for Mom's stove and some bathroom handlebars to install so Mom could get in and out of the tub chair easily. Then, I showed up at the hospital with more Eastwood and Carol Burnett videos.

Mom was actually hungry; but for once, I didn't bring anything. I went downstairs and picked her up some chicken strips and fries. She ate about one before the hospital lunch arrived. She ate the Jell-O and tried to eat another chicken strip. I stayed for a while, but we both were pretty quiet. Her roommate was cranky and fussy and had a lot of company. I left around 4:00 and Mom asked me to bring her some Chinese food, without MSG, tomorrow.

It was still early and the weather wasn't bad, so I drove around for about an hour, too bored to go back to the house. I went to Target, just to browse, and made it home an hour later. I put in a call to Hubby, but there was no answer. I so miss him and my home. I then called Tonya and talked to her for a bit. Her youngest was sick so she was tending to her. I didn't keep her on the phone long.

Finally, I got home and tried to fix the handles on the stove, but it required different screws. Oh, well, back to Lowe's.

13

MORE BAD NEWS...AND
THEN SOME GOOD

February 7ᵗʰ through February 9ᵗʰ, 2005

I had some horrible dreams and woke up constantly throughout the night. I finally got up around 8:30 a.m. with a splitting headache. It was pouring rain. Mom had not called, so I watched TV for a bit until the *only* MSG-free Chinese restaurant in Fort Wayne opened. I called in our order at 10:30 and headed out to get it, all the while reliving the crazy dreams I had during the night.

I called Seveda on my drive back to the hospital and she helped calm me down from my horrible dreams. She said it's normal to have funky dreams. Mine involved Mom running away from me, hobbling with her walker and even falling, but for some reason I could not catch up with her. Then, her face appeared in front of me almost like a death mask. I woke up scared and out of breath.

I arrived at the hospital just before noon to find Mom highly agitated. Her troubled 101-year-old roommate, Eva, was surrounded by physical therapists, and their butts were in the divider curtain, crowding near Mom's face! Apparently, Eva had cried most of the night and kept Mom from sleeping. Shoot…maybe she had the same scary dreams I had!

Mom hates to take drugs, let alone a sleeping pill, but I suggested she might have to tonight so she could get some sleep. Eva was used to having company all the time, even when she was at the nursing home, so when she's alone, she has fits. Well, Mom was fit to be tied, but happy to see that I remembered the Chinese food. We ate and tried to ignore the commotion going on in the bed next to us.

When Mom went to her first occupational therapy session, I called the nurses and asked them to move Eva's bed closer to the window and to remove the extra chair from beside the curtain, as it was overcrowding Mom. The room is quite small for two people, but Nurse Debra met my requests. Now, if only Eva would just sleep through the night!

Nurse Debra told me that Mom was nauseous and did not eat much this morning. She did not fare too well in her first occupational therapy (OT) session either, and was not looking forward to the radiation treatment.

At radiation, we met with Dr. Trenkner's associate, Dr. Apple, who went over Mom's progress since her treatment began. He said it's too soon to see any changes in the tumor, but her red blood count had dropped to 8.8; it was 9.0 last week. A normal red blood count should be 14.0. He said Mom would need to build up her red cells to feel better and to tolerate any chemo she may undertake.

Dr. Apple had a calm and soothing manner, and I think, for the first time, *Mom was listening*. Dr. Apple indicated that she could boost her red cell count via a transfusion or via an injection of Procrit. Mom asked if adding supplements to her diet would help, as she was not in favor of a blood transfusion, or any injection, for that matter. Dr. Apple informed her that those types of supplements could take up to sixty days to make a difference in her system. He again simply explained how the tumors in her liver, *and* lungs, *and* lymph nodes would continue to eat away at the red cells, and that chemo would destroy them. He offered that he realized she was apprehensive about chemo and a transfusion, but added that the risk of infection is almost *nil* in this region. As far as the chemo, he said Mom could try it for two sessions to see how she reacted to it, and could quit anytime if she didn't care for it. He suggested that Dr. Carr would be able to see how well the chemo was working on the tumors after two sessions.

Mom asked what her lungs would feel like if she did nothing. Dr. Apple said that at first, she would feel winded, but as the tumor grew, it could break through the walls of her lungs, causing bleeding and blood clots. As for her liver, it would decrease its ability to filter her blood and eventually shut down, killing her. He said Mom's lack of appetite would continue to decline, and she'd continue to lose weight.

He explained that while it was great that she's undergoing radiation treatments for her hip, those treatments would mean nothing if she didn't fix the bigger problem. He related that it was like fixing a dent on a car, but doing nothing to fix the engine. Since the engine runs the car as a whole, it would eventually break down, regardless of the dent in its side. Mom looked at him and seriously considered doing the blood transfusion and two sessions of chemo! I, on the other hand, crumbled inside; my heart was breaking.

I cannot emphasize how much I appreciated Dr. Apple. He was very cool and totally "got" my mother. He said he could set up the chemo sessions before she was released from the hospital this week. After we saw him, we ran into Dr. Trenkner's nurse, Mary, and we told her what Dr. Apple had suggested. She said Dr. T was not too concerned about Mom's low red cell count, but if Mom was going to pursue chemo, she could set up a transfusion for tomorrow after consulting with Dr. T.

Back in her hospital room, Mom was a bit hungry and tired. I hung around after heating up her Chinese food and oiled her arms down with the eucalyptus oil, as her skin was dry. I left early that evening so I could make a run to see Aunt Mable. I kissed Mommy goodbye and told her to try to get some rest.

Aunt Mable looked good – she was in her new room, but without her new roomie. She was watching TV, as usual, and was about to be taken down to dinner. I helped her empty out her bags – cards, tapes, a calendar – and hung them on the wall. She asked about Mom, and when she would be going home. I told her this week, but Mom was still giving the doctors a hard time. Aunt Mable laughed and recalled the times over the years when Mom was stubborn.

I walked Auntie down to the dinner area and sat with her while the attendants passed out coffee and water. Suddenly, I felt an overwhelming sadness at the sight of all the patients there, and could not stay any longer. I lied and said I had to get back home due to the rain and darkness, and would see her soon. Sweet Auntie gave me the biggest kiss as I hugged her goodbye.

I cried like a big baby when I reached the car. It's just not right to watch the ones you love grow so helpless and alone. It just breaks my heart. My entire family seemed to be slipping away from me and there was nothing I could do about it. I drove over to Lowe's to return one of the towel bars and to get a phone cord to lengthen the one in Mom's bedroom. I felt so teary walking around the store, and again cried uncontrollably all the way home. I wish I could stop crying; I don't have cancer and I'm sure Mom is more scared than I can imagine. I so wish I could do something more. I'm so afraid to go back to Pasadena and leave Mom, but I miss my Hubby, our home, our dog. God help me through this so I can be strong for Mom and Aunt Mable!

That night I, once again, laid awake until about 3:00 a.m. I just can't seem to fall asleep. I woke up around 8:30 the next morning but didn't lag around the house. It was still raining, damn…but I need to pay a bill, go to the post office, and drop off paperwork to Project Renew. Gregor let me be myself last night – I cried uncontrollably during our phone call. Poor guy, I know he can't stand it when I cry, but he was the best, as usual. He said all the right things and made me feel loved. God, how I miss him!

I completed my errands and stopped by Denny's to pick up an omelet and some coffee for Mom. When I arrived at the hospital, Mom was annoyed again, due to Eva making gagging noises while she was trying to eat her breakfast. It took Mom's already poor appetite away, though she liked the smell of the coffee and eggs and did try to eat a bit.

Mom said she slept well, in spite of her weepy roommate, due to taking a sleeping pill. She said she felt great and rested. She only had two OT sessions today because the therapy department had meetings scheduled for the afternoon. We chilled and watched TV until it was time for the guys to take us to radiation therapy. We did ask Nurse Debra if she had heard any word concerning the blood transfusion. She knew nothing of it, but would check into it after I explained what Dr. Apple had discovered from Mom's blood test results.

Radiation went well. Lee said that after Mom goes home, he would be willing to check in on her free of charge. I know he works two jobs and seems to have a busy life, so I'm not sure I would want to impose upon him. Still, it was real nice of him to offer – that dang Hoosier Hospitality!

Back at the hospital, the nurse came in and gave Mom a TB test to make sure she did not contract anything while in the hospital. *Really?* That's all she needed, an infection from this place – I was not happy, but they would check Mom's arm before she is released. I then re-heated the omelet from earlier for Mom to snack on. I knew she must be hungry, or at least I hoped she was. Mom ate very little today, but did crave a chocolate milkshake. Turns out, we could request one for her from the nurse and they would make one and bring it to her. I put in a request and they brought her a small one a few minutes later. She was craving a pineapple shake, so I'll bring her one from Dairy Queen tomorrow.

I left around 5:00 p.m. and drove to Big K to get some vitamin D with calcium as per Dr. Apple's suggestion. I also began to shop for items for her to eat once she goes home. Looks like I will need to do a major shopping trip tomorrow at Scott's. I figured I'd also need to go by the Cancer Services Center tomorrow to get her a walker without wheels, since that's what she's used to using at the hospital. The one at the house (Aunt Mable's) has wheels. Back at the house, I fixed the light above the sink and took out the trash.

Gregor called while I was at Big K. He was driving around in the wonderfully warm Pasadena sun thinking of me. I can't wait to get back! I then called Shirley, who was out and has no voicemail. *Ugh!!* I'm so glad I got her that cell phone so I could reach her or leave a message when I needed to. Anyway, she called back later that evening and we discussed Mom's situation. She's still willing to come by twice a week to check in on Mom, as she does not have classes on Monday or Friday. I asked her to take the cell phone instead of reaching me via her phone cards, and she said she would.

Cousin Shirley meant well, but she kept insisting that I convince Mom to have someone move in with her. I again explained to her that Mom would never go for that, now or *ever*! I told her again that Mom was hell-bent on being at home, by herself, to tend to herself like she used to. Shirley backed down and said she understood. I will try to schedule Mom's doctor appointments on days Shirley is available so she can take her, since Mom cannot drive herself. If that is not possible, I will speak with the folks at Cancer Services to set up transportation for her follow-up appointments with Dr. Gertsen and Dr. Carr.

Shirley said she would come by on Friday to see us and coordinate all the appointments for her. I felt bad for being so crabby. She is such a centered, dear person who could see I was stressed and did not take my funky mood personally. She's a good soul. I'm grateful for her help and will try to be stronger around her.

The next morning, I woke up to discover that it was *snowing again*! What the hell? Looks like there's already about four inches on the ground, with even more to come. Mom called and told me not to come due to the snow. Yeah, right, I don't think so. I told her I would be there by noon. She sounded tired and complained that Eva was up all night again, and even though Mom took sleeping pills, she could not get any rest. The staff had been in and out of the room all night tending to Eva.

Mom said she called for another sleeping pill and wanted to forego OT this morning to get some rest. She was also again very nauseous, and has taken a pill for that. I'll get her that pineapple shake and some fries on my way in.

I stopped first at Cancer Services and got services expedited to get her a walker. I then went to Dairy Queen and picked up the shake. I arrived in Mom's room before 11:30, but she looked unusually fatigued. She got no rest last night, felt very sick to her stomach, and had no appetite. She was fighting sleep, so I convinced her to take a nap. I spoke briefly with the OT therapist, Rachel, who said we really needed to get Mom on the stairs today so she would be ready for the stairs at home. She was going to try working with Mom again after her radiation this afternoon.

I've not seen Mom look or feel this bad since she was admitted. At one point, when she came back from the bathroom, she sat upright for a second and then just fell over, collapsing on the bed! She's never done that before. She seemed so exhausted from just going to the bathroom. I spoke to the nurse, who said they had given her pills for the nausea, but there was not much more they could do.

The final session of radiation went well and we saw Dr. Trenkner's nurse, Mary, right before Mom went in. She said that after speaking with Dr. T and telling him what Dr. Apple said, he indicated that under no uncertain terms does Mom need a transfusion at this time. While Mom's red cells were lower than 8.8 two weeks ago, they went up to 9.0 on their own.

We were told that Dr. Apple really had no business alerting us to this since he did not know Mom's full medical history, and that he had unnecessarily concerned us with his talk of transfusion. Even if she underwent chemo, it could be done safely with her red cells at 8.8. Damn! Mom had this look like, "*See, I told you so, doctors don't know everything!*"

What could I say? This was one man's opinion, and thankfully, we hadn't gone through the procedure. Nurse Mary also indicated that the radiation could be adding to Mom's fatigue, and that she might also be coming down with a virus. Damn, like we need yet another problem to deal with! Back in her room, Mom felt increasingly weak. I have no way of helping her, and feel so helpless. She looks so uncomfortable and in need of relief.

Her roomie had been unruly all day. If, for some odd reason, Mom has to stay past tomorrow, I will request a room change. She has to get some sleep, and all the fussing, noise, and ruckus Eva causes is quite disruptive to my mother.

Mom drank some of her milkshake and seemed to enjoy it. She tried to have a bowel movement to no avail, though she seems to feel that if she poops or vomits she'll feel better. I left her for a minute to get a salad, only to come back to find Mom asleep. Nurse Debra said it was okay for me to sit in the lounge while she slept.

I hung out for about thirty minutes when Rachel returned mid-afternoon to encourage Mom to try walking up and down the stairs. However, when Mom came out of the bathroom this time, she just collapsed when she reached the bed. Rachel was concerned that she may not be able to release Mom if she did not attempt to work the stairs. She saw Mom's status had not changed since this morning and took her pulse and clipped a small instrument to her finger to measure her blood oxygen. Her pulse was 165, just from walking from the bathroom to her bed! Her blood oxygen was about 95. Rachel and the nurse said they usually gave oxygen to someone when levels fell to 94. The nurse on call soon came in and took her temperature, which was 99 degrees, and her blood pressure was 104 over 70. They went ahead and gave her pills for pain and nausea, and would give her another pain pill around 10:00 p.m. so she could sleep through the night.

I told them there was too much activity through the night in her room, which was why she is so fatigued. They understood, and would work on keeping Eva up during the day so she would sleep during the night. Rachel told me she would put in a request to have Mom get OT in the morning to work the stairs, and would also put in a request for therapy for when she goes home.

Ideally, she wants Mom to get therapy in her home, but Mom refuses – *"They're always late and I can't wait around for them,"* she told Rachel. There's nothing anyone can do about folks being late, but she does know that if Mom does not continue with therapy, she will not get better and off the walker!

Nurse Debra said she spoke with Dr. Carr's nurse, Margaret, who would stop by tomorrow morning and give me Mom's schedule for her future appointments with Dr. Carr. The pain pills hit Mom pretty quickly, and she soon fell asleep. I stayed until about 5:30 to make sure they did not disturb her for bullshit reasons – eating, tests, etc. The staff could see I was not feeling them and they kept their distance until I needed them. I kissed the sleepy lady goodbye as she tried to fuss at me about staying with her too long.

I just drove and drove. I felt so helpless, so lost, so alone in all of this. I ended up at Scott's and picked up some food for Mom to enjoy and cook in the microwave when she gets home.

14

FREE AT LAST...FREE AT LAST

February 10th, 2005

I awoke bright and early and got to the hospital before 9:00 a.m. Mom was relaxing and looked one hundred percent better than she had yesterday. *Thank God!* She had her occupational therapy work on the stairs scheduled for 10:30. I packed up all her stuff and Mom got dressed on her own. What a difference a day made. She had more energy and looked less tired. She'd slept all night and didn't hear anything out of Eva. Thank you, Lord!

Mom worked up a sweat in OT. She did the stairs with the therapist and then with me about three times. She also did quite a few leg raises with one-pound weights and did a "lap" around the gym. She really looked tired at the end when I pushed her back into her room.

Mom had no appetite for her lunch, but did drink her Ensure shake. Rhonda, the home services nurse, came in and told us PT would begin on Monday. They will call to let us know what time they would be coming by the house, three times a week. After that, Mom could get more therapy as an outpatient at any place we like. I waited for Mom to fire a barb at her about this, but luckily, she remained quiet!

Nurse Debra stopped by to let us know that Margaret, Dr. Carr's nurse, would be stopping by around 1:00 to answer any last questions we may have and to let us know about our next appointment for the chemo assessment. She would also print out all the medication Mom will be sent home with, and write down all of her appointments with her three doctors. Debra's been one of the best nurses ever, so Mom gave her the plant she received as a gift from one of her friends. After all, Mom admits she would only kill it if she brought it home.

Lunch was served, but was nasty as ever – how do you screw up fried chicken? We watched soaps and waited for the discharge paperwork to be completed. Finally, Nurse Margaret showed up (after I had to get Debra to page her), and she explained what would happen at the February 21st appointment. She would see Dr. Carr for chemo assessment. If her red cells were below 8.0, they would set her up to do a transfusion at the radiation center. If her white cells were low, she would get a shot of some type of statin to level her out. The process to test her blood was called a "Nadir Count". Mom could have her first treatment as early as the following day if her blood tests were fine. Then, she would have another Nadir Count done ten days after her treatment to check her blood levels.

Throughout our meeting with the hospital staff, Cousin Mildred kept calling to see if we had left yet. She wants to stop by the house to see Mom once she knows we're on our way. I explained we were in the process of being discharged and that I would call her once we arrived home.

After what seemed like hours, the volunteers finally came and Debra had our discharge printouts, at-home instructions, and prescriptions. Debra would have Dr. Wallace call in a prescription for an antibiotic to help clear up a slight infection Mom has in her bladder.

All of Mom's medications have no refills. She had one for iron pills, one for pain pills, and one for an antibiotic, each with a 30-day supply. That seemed odd. Would Mom have to re-visit the doctor to get refills, or what? Mom was also supposed to take 325mg of aspirin and a stool softener daily.

I pulled the anteater-mobile to the front of the hospital and loaded Mom in. She was happy, as was I, to get out of that hospital. At the house, she made it up the porch stairs slowly and without too much difficulty. It was great to see her walk back into her house and start fussing about all the changes, although slight, that I had made. *"She's baaack!"* I thought to myself, smiling. When Mildred arrived shortly after, I left to fill Mom's prescriptions.

It was a quiet evening. Gregor called and talked with Mom; she couldn't wait to jokingly fuss to him about how bossy I've been and how I needed to get back to Pasadena. You could tell she was getting tired and was soon ready to go to bed. I tried to get her to drink more water since she was so dehydrated, but it backfired. After she took her last pill for iron, she threw up, mostly water, in front of the sofa.

Mom felt really bad as I cleaned up and made her bed ready. I told her she really needed to stop worrying about me taking care of her. I told her I loved her and she meant more to me than anything in the world. Besides, I reminded her that she wiped up enough vomit and poop of mine when I was a baby. She laughed and walked on to bed.

Mom got up around 9:00 that evening. She said she needed a pain pill but was afraid to take one for fear of throwing up. I told her she probably had too much water in her earlier, but now she was empty and it should be okay to take one. She took one without any problem and had a bowel movement too, which was great since she's had such a tough time with elimination. I only hope she sleeps through the night.

Mom woke up around 3:00 a.m. needing to pee, and was able to do so without too much difficulty. I had left the bathroom light on with the door cracked just so she would not have to reach to turn it on. She went back to bed but then asked to take her acid reducer pill – she had thrown it up before going to bed. I gave her one, plus an antibiotic and she went back to sleep until about 8:45 a.m. Not bad.

In the morning, Mom seemed a bit sluggish, but was able to go to the bathroom. I suggested a shower and a change of clothes, which she did pretty much on her own. I decided to cook up all the turkey bacon to store away in the fridge for later, as she only wanted toast with peanut butter for breakfast. I fixed that for her, as well as some apple juice. She only ate a couple of bites, but drank all the juice. Mom claimed she didn't need a pain pill, but I asked her to take one to stay ahead of the pain, along with the iron pill and two of her four aspirin.

Cousin Mildred called to say she was on her way over with some homemade chili – Mom swears it's the best. Tonya also called, saying she had just pulled up in front of the house, bearing the rest of the Girl Scout cookies I had ordered for Aunt Mable. I let her in and she, Mom, and I chatted up a storm while I continued to cook the bacon.

Mildred got to the house before noon and Mom grew more animated. She started complaining to Mildred that I was *"hovering"* too much; I was being *"bossy"*; I was *"this"*, I was not *"that"*, etc., etc., which began to piss me off. I thought, *"Really Mom? Where's your fucking perfect son? And who's cleaning up your vomit and shit?"* Ugh! Okay, *breathe, Nat, breathe*…this is just her way of coping, I tried to convince myself. Sorry, I digress…

Mildred heated up some of the chili for the two of them while I wrote in the journal I had begun yesterday. It contained all of Mom's appointments, phone contacts, Doctor's names and numbers, as well as the phone numbers of Shirley, Mildred (sometimes Mom forgets it), Linda, and mine. I also created a calendar showing her appointments with each doctor for February 16th, 21st and March 10th. I hung it up close to Mom in the living room so when she's on the phone she would have easy reference to when and where her next appointment was, and with whom.

Every day when she's on the phone, she talks about her appointments, but cannot remember which is which. Despite her complaining about me being *"overly organized"* and treating her like a disabled person, I continued to make my notes so whoever comes over to check on her will have easy access to what's going on.

Cousin Shirley was late coming over, but called around 1:00 that afternoon, citing she had some running to do but would be over in about thirty minutes. When she did arrive, we spoke for a bit and then I left to get keys made for her. When I returned, she and Mom were talking it up. Shirley was taking notes about Mom's appointments. She was also discussing if Mom liked "juicing". Mom told her she had an old juice machine that I found behind some pots in the kitchen cabinet.

Shirley said she wanted to start Mom on fresh-made juices and made me a list of vegetables she wanted me to pick up. She indicated she would be back over on Sunday after church to make juices for Mom. Shirley seems to have a spiritual sense about her that Mom seems cool with. Although she fought me, she took the cell phone I purchased for her. I showed her how to use it and that I already put in the phone numbers for Mom, Mildred, and all of my contact numbers.

After she left, I needed to run to Kinko's to fax paperwork for Aunt Mable's Medicare eligibility. Hesitantly, I left Mom alone for the first time since her release. After I was finished at Kinko's, I ran to Wal-Mart to pick up the veggies Shirley indicated so I would not have to go tomorrow. I also picked up a heating pad for Mom. She's been complaining that her back and waist hurt, but did not want me to get anything for her.

Back home, Mom was doing okay; she was still stretched out on the sofa, but said she had gotten up to pee without difficulty. She looked like she had more energy today, but still gets winded after walking a short distance. I wet the moisture pad that came with the heating pad and put it on

Mom's back. It has an auto-off switch that shuts down after one hour, so it's perfect for Mom, since she likes to overdo it and keep the bloody thing on all night.

Gregor and Linda called later in the evening; I told them how Mom was doing. Greg spoke with Mom for a few minutes, but Mom was getting sleepy. Afterward, she took her meds without any trouble – no vomiting tonight – and a pain pill so she would not wake up during the night. I ran another load of clothes, and after we sorted out more of her bills, Mom went to bed early.

15

DO I LEAVE OR DO I STAY?

Saturday, February 12th, 2005

D amn, even with Mom here, I still have a hard time falling asleep. I'm also torn about leaving Mom. I finally drifted off around 3:00 a.m. Mom woke up around 5:00 needing to pee and could not fall back to sleep. I gave her the remote for that bedroom's TV, but she couldn't find anything on that she wanted to watch. She had unplugged her heating pad, so I had to turn it around and add an extension cord to avoid this happening after I'm gone.

I drifted back to sleep and woke up around 8:30 a.m. Mom was rising too, and she had a bit more pep in her step today. She even went into the kitchen and poured herself some OJ from the fridge! She went to pee and changed her clothes while in the bathroom, without my help. Wow, this was so nice to see.

I wanted to run out and get Mom a second heating pad so she would not have to unplug the one from the bedroom and carry it to plug it in behind the sofa in the living room. I know she'll fuss when she sees that I got it, but too bad.

I went into one last task mode. I made it to see Aunt Mable first, to say goodbye and to let her talk to Mom via my cell phone. Check. I also had another set of keys made for Linda, which Mom was cool with. Check. I stopped by Big K and picked up another heating pad and a large number universal remote for that second TV. Check and double check. Mom had been fussing that the remote that came with the television was too small for her to see, let alone figure out.

Mom looked good when I got back to the house, but she did fuss when I showed her the second heating pad. I had also picked up more bottled water for her; she needs to keep hydrated and it's better than drinking soda pop.

Mildred soon called and asked Mom if I was really going back to California. Mom repeated Mildred's question just as I walked past her.

Damn, what the hell does Mildred mean by that, and why the hell did Mom feel a need to repeat it? Mom told her I was leaving at 2:00 that afternoon. I know Mom needs to exert her independence, but now I can't help feeling I'm doing the wrong thing by leaving. Folks who feel the need to add their own opinion about my staying or leaving don't help matters either. Still, I need to get back to take care of my Hubby and my job. In addition, I cannot continue to sleep on Mom's couch; it's killing my back.

If I stayed here, I'd have to get my own place and a job. That, for now, is out of the question. If Project Renew would move things along quicker, then my own place could be right next-door. Unfortunately, it needs a total rehab just to make it livable. I must let Mom make her way without my constant teary smile and stares. I know she hates being in this kind of pain and uncertainty, and I can only imagine her frustration.

Mildred came by to sit with Mom, and Linda came by about an hour later to take me to the airport. I made one last check around the house to make sure all plans, food, and folks were in place. Mom, of course, was annoyed with me doing that. Maybe it *is* time for me to leave – we really do get on each other's nerves and we were closing in on our "three-day curve"! I had left some money in Mom's wallet but I wouldn't tell her about it until I got back to Pasadena. I hugged and kissed Mom and gave busybody Mildred an obligatory hug. Time to fly.

I reached the airport, still filled with uncertainly as to whether I should stay or go. Tonya even called to see if I was really going to leave – *what the hell is wrong with everyone?* Deep down I know I am making the right decision for *me*, for now, because we are just getting in each other's way and on each other's nerves. I have lots of support for Mom in place, and I do plan on coming back in a few weeks, barring what my job has to say about it. I made the mistake of asking Linda if I was wrong for leaving – she made no comment one way or the other, but I could also tell she thinks I should stay. *Damn...*

My plane was delayed forty-five minutes, which made gave me only fifteen minutes to make my connection in Dallas. I ran like Tom Cruise through their airport; thank God for their tram, which got me to the gate with only five minutes to spare. I called Gregor from the plane and told him I had made it, and to expect me at the scheduled arrival time of 7:00 p.m.

It was great seeing my Hubby, our home, and our dog. There's a sense of peace and calm here. I melted into my Hubby's arms and we remained embraced through the night, with our little dog curled up at my feet.

16

BACK IN CALIFORNIA

February 14ᵗʰ through February 19ᵗʰ, 2005

I called Mom upon my return to California, and have been checking in with her and Shirley daily. She sounds good and insists I need to stop worrying about her. I began to get back into my routine and work. I'm up at 6:00 a.m. and have to be to work by 6:45. It's so weird being back here; the weather, the mountains...all so strange. Being back at work is weird too. Everyone was so curious as to where I've been. Some who did know cornered me to ask about Mom.

I was holding it together pretty well until my boss, Laura, asked me about Mom, and then I just lost it. Gretchen gave me a hug, which made even more water flow. Chase was real nice too, and had just asked about Mom when my cell phone rang – it was Mom! I turned off the ringer and went into one of the long hallways to take the call. She never calls during the day. Oh God, I prayed, no bad news please!

Mom sounded tired, but was calling to tell me that the physical therapist was going to come by the house today just after lunch. She also felt the need to tell me that she had two bowel movements... *TMI, Mom!* What a funny lady. She was really trying to sound upbeat, but I could hear the weariness in her voice. I told her I was at work and all was great, and that I would call her back that afternoon.

The day went fast; I got teary a couple of times, but held it together. Barbara asked me to eat lunch with her, but I felt like going for a drive. She spoke with me for a bit, and convinced me to stay and have lunch with her. Barbara really understands what I'm going through since she is a cancer survivor.

I called Mom back during my afternoon break. The therapist answered the phone and was still going through the intake process – a bunch of paperwork. I called back around 6:00 in the evening, Ft. Wayne time, and Mom was already in bed. She said she was exhausted and Mildred had just left. I didn't keep her on the phone long, but told her I loved her and wished her sweet dreams.

When I got home, it dawned on me that I totally forgot it was Valentine's Day – but not my Hubby! I came home to flowers, a beautiful card, and dinner reservations at one of our favorite Mexican spots. We had a nice time, stayed off the subject of Mom, and spent the rest of the evening at home snuggling and making out.

Exhaustion had finally caught up with me because I ended up oversleeping. How did I totally ignore the damn alarm? I sprang out of bed at 6:30 a.m., and did not leave the house until 7:00. Traffic was a pain today – not like the smooth ride in yesterday.

I felt cranky at work – some stupid, though well-meaning heifer, tried to soothe me by saying, *"Things will get better"* with my mother. Uh, *no they won't,* I thought. I ended up snapping back at her, *"When this thing is done with my Mom, she will be gone – how is that better?"* Damn…those words slipped out when they were meant to be just a thought. I didn't mean to snap at her, but her statement, combined with my lack of sleep, had me in a shitty mood all day.

I drove around for lunch and did not eat, but instead drove to Target and found a pillow for my hard-ass chair at work. I found out after the fact from Barbara that our supervisor, Darrin, could have ordered one out of our catalog for no cost, so I asked him to please order one for me and returned the one I bought after work.

I called Mom during my second break. She said Shirley was over today juicing for her, but she had no appetite – still. She sees Dr. Gertsen tomorrow for the hip and Dr. Carr on Monday. She asked about Hubby and Zorro and tried to make conversation, but again, I could tell she was very tired and not feeling well at all. I gave her my love and let her go. I then left a message for Shirley to call me about how Mom looked today.

Shirley called around 6:00 that evening after I got home from work. She confirmed that Mom had felt sluggish and was not eating as much as she should. She asked how I was doing and I, of course, lied and said I was okay.

The next morning, I woke up to such a beautiful day. The sun rose against the San Gabriel Mountains as I was driving in to work. I had also enjoyed a full, restful night of sleep. I approached the day with an upbeat attitude and decided to call Mom during my morning break. She sounded great – much better than yesterday. She said her appointment with Dr. Gertsen went well, and he told her the hip was on the mend. Monday's appointment with Dr. Carr will be the real test as to how she's doing. Mom's PT and OT therapists will be coming by tomorrow. Linda called, she said, and Shirley came by on her way to school yesterday.

Mom said she's still tired all the time and is now spending most of her time in bed after company leaves. Mildred spends quite a bit of time visiting and bringing Mom home-cooked food. Mom still has no appetite. She got up last night to pee and went to get a drink of water, but threw it up on her way back to bed. She just can't understand why she can't keep anything down. I told her that we loved her and would check in on her tomorrow to see how the therapy went.

The next day, I woke up tired and achy. It's humid out and a bit overcast; rain is predicted today... ugh! Work was busy as ever; I seemed to come back late from every break I had today. I called Mom during my evening break since Mom's PT and OT had been scheduled that afternoon. I reached Mom around 6:00 in the evening, her time, and she was lying in bed watching TV. She said the two therapists did come by today, despite the snow that fell through the night. She said they really worked her and she was very tired. Shirley also came by and had made her more celery and beet juice (yuck). Mom seems to love it and said she drinks it all up.

I did not keep her long since she sounded so tired, so I told her Gregor and I loved her and would speak with her tomorrow. It soon started to rain, which pretty much matched my mood after speaking with her. Tomorrow, Gregor's sister, Lynn, was coming into town to visit us for the weekend. I hope the weather breaks so she can have a good time touring around and seeing the sights. I'll try not to be too much of a party pooper.

Lynn got into town late Thursday night, and she and Gregor stayed up late talking and catching up. I tipped around quietly the next morning as I slipped out for work; it was another bloody, rainy day. I spoke with Mom that evening, and she sounded good but tired. Shirley had been by again to make her some more juice – she hated the one she made with spinach. I told her Zorro has an "audition" with a pet acting management company. She laughed and commented how wild our dog is and how he will be a mess. I agreed, but thought it would be fun to check out. It was good to hear Mom laugh.

Saturday morning, I got up early and finished Zorro's "pup"-folio for the audition. Gregor was a real trooper and went with us. He knew the building location and, fortunately, the rains began to subside by the time we got there. This thing was such a trip; Zorro was fine for a while, but when it came time to sit down as a group with twelve other owners and their dogs, he began that clingy thing he does, like when he hears a truck backing up.

The two tricks he did know went out the window as his fur flew everywhere while he tried to climb over my back to exit the room. Of course, we had sat up front to make sure he was seen…ugh; not a good plan since he was acting fearful of the agent's voice.

In spite of his behavior, the salesperson "determined" that he would be *perfect* for their Level One plan – and how lucky we were to be offered this opportunity as Zorro, *"has such a nice face and great potential!"* Yeah, they laid it on thick – almost like those time-share hard sells without the bullshit. We were then corralled into an office and given the spiel on the program/workshop Zorro would be eligible for. As she put it, for a mere, *"Seventy-eight-ninety-five,"* Zorro could get, *"the best discipline training, headshots, and opportunities in the world."* The salesperson then pushed the contract toward me to review and sign.

Now, mind you, Hubby was just sitting back and not saying a word throughout all of this. I looked over at him, confused by his silence, and then back at the salesperson. I told her we would have to go home and discuss this before we signed any contract. Again, nothing from Hubby. Now the salesperson chimed in again, about how great this opportunity was, etc., etc., etc. I stopped her by citing my mother was very ill right now and that our funds had been diverted toward that end. She said she understood and took Zorro's composite photos to file away.

When we left the building, I said to Gregor, *"They have got to be out of their fucking minds!"* He didn't know why I hesitated, as *"eighty dollars"* was not too much to pay for obedience classes. What? *Halt… stop… hold it right there… eighty dollars?* I explained to Gregor that the contract said it was going to cost seven *thousand*, eight hundred ninety-five dollars! Gregor's mouth dropped. He was definitely having a "duh" moment. We cracked up about this for the rest of the day – and for these few moments, we relaxed and did not worry about how sick Mom was.

Once we got home, we called Mom and shared with her the Zorro "audition" experience. She laughed up a storm. Mom also wanted to speak with Gregor, and they had a nice, lengthy conversation. Afterward, he felt torn as to how much he should impose his views on what she should do regarding the chemo. I told him to put it back on her and just listen to what she had to say. I told him to not feel pressed to try and "fix" the matter for her. Let her say what she wants.

On Sunday morning, I decided to cook breakfast for Hubby and his sister, Lynn. The rain had stopped and we all hung out and spent the day together. The next thing I knew, it was too late to call Mom. *Am I a bad daughter or what?* Damn, I'll check with her in the morning on my way to work.

I was able to speak with Mom the next morning while driving in the pouring rain to work. She sounded a bit tired, but in good spirits. Mildred was there and had made her some oatmeal. She was upset with herself because she still does not have much of an appetite. I reminded her that the nausea and lack of appetite would come back to her, and then reminded her of her 3:15 appointment with Dr. Carr today. She said she and Mildred were all set, and the people who would be picking them up would be by at 2:30.

Mom then complained that she had been trying to call me on my cell last week without any luck. I told her that was odd, as my cell was always on, but we could not figure out why she was unable to get through. She said she had tried the operator, who told her the circuits were busy.

We finished our conversation by the time I arrived at work. A few minutes later, my cell rang – it was Mom, trying my phone to see if she could get through. I told her again that I loved her and would talk to her after her appointment with Dr. Carr. I then called Dr. Carr and left a message for him to call me after his meeting with Mom so I could be updated on what's going on.

17

MORE BAD NEWS...GOTTA GO BACK

February 21st, 2005

It continued to *rain, rain, rain* in Los Angeles; so much so a tree in one of the parking lots at my job fell on a couple of employee's cars. Thank God mine was not hit. During lunch, the rain slowed down, so I went out to my car to have some quiet time. While I sat in the car, my phone rang. It was Shirley, informing me that she and Mildred were with Mom in the ER. Mom had been feeling bad and weak and couldn't breathe.

I spoke with Mildred, who said she had been at the house and could see Mom was in distress. Mom was asked if she wanted to go to the hospital; she said yes and the ambulance quickly came and took her in. The hospital was now running tests, giving her blood, and would most likely admit her. Shirley said Mom did not look good and that I should get back to Fort Wayne. I told Shirley I would be on the earliest plane back to Indiana.

I ran back inside my job and found my boss, who I pulled to the side. I started to cry as I told him what had happened and that I needed to leave now. He told me to go and to not worry about the job.

I called Gregor as I sped home and told him what was going on. By the time I got home, his sister was packing to leave. She gave her regards to my Mom and said she would keep us in her prayers. I then searched for a flight to Indiana – first for both Gregor and I, and then just for me. It didn't make sense for both of us to go. We would have to board the dog and all the places were closed today since it was a holiday. Perhaps deep down, I feared if Gregor did go, that would mean Mom was going to die…I didn't want to jinx it. I found a good one-way fare through United, contacted Shirley and Linda with the details and left Gordon a message.

Dr. Carr called me around 3:30 as per my request. He knew Mom was in the hospital after he tried to reach her after she missed her appointment. His colleague, Dr. Whelan, had called him, as he was attending to her in Parkview's ER. He said they were going to give her blood to get her energy back up and then do an MRI on her stomach area. It appears the cancer may have spread into her intestinal region. Also, because her breathing was labored, she might have pneumonia, but they would know more after they run their tests.

Later in the evening, I called Parkview and got Mom's room number. I tried to call her, but there was no answer. Shirley called around 5:00 that evening from Mom's room. She said Mom looked tired but was getting a Heparin drip with an IV saline solution. Shirley put Mom on the phone and we spoke briefly, as she was pretty drugged up. I told her I was coming home and would see her tomorrow. She managed to fuss at me about coming back, but I just blew her kisses and told her I loved her.

Tuesday, February 22nd - Back to Ft. Wayne...

Restless, I woke up at 4:00 a.m. the next morning, unable to go back to sleep. Both Gregor and Zorro were knocked out. It was pouring rain and the thunder soon brought Zorro into our bed. After snuggling with Hubby, I got up and got dressed. I figured I would go downstairs and work on our taxes. Gregor got up with the alarm at 5:30 and we left for LAX soon thereafter. I made it to Ft. Wayne by 6:15 that evening.

Linda is such a dear person. She called and told me she would pick me up at the airport so I wouldn't have to take a cab. She was there waiting as I got off the plane. She drove me to Mom's house, where I dropped off my bag and got the keys to the anteater-mobile. Linda then followed me to the hospital to visit Mom and to get the real deal as to what's going on.

Mom was asleep and looked drawn and in pain, so we left the room to find her nurse. No one could be found. Finally, we asked one aide walking around for Mom's nurse. The aide was on her way home – it was shift change time – but she was kind enough to get Mom's chart for us. Mom had had a CT scan done and there were blockages of her bile duct – the vessel that connects the gallbladder to the liver and lets bile go through. They are going to go in tomorrow to put a shunt in her to open it up.

She also has jaundice because of this blockage, and her skin appears yellow. The aide told us Dr. Whelan would be around tomorrow to answer any questions we might have. They have Mom on a Heparin drip for her blood and an IV of saline to keep her hydrated.

Linda and I went back into the room and woke Mom up. She looked so tired and complained about having dry lips and mouth. She fussed about the food, which made us laugh, but she was really fighting sleep. I kissed her goodbye and went back to the house. During the drive to the house, I couldn't help but feel odd about being back in Fort Wayne. The house was clean, empty, and quite haunting. Hope I can sleep tonight.

Wednesday, February 23rd - Those Yellow Eyes…
Mom called at 6:30 in the morning, asking me to bring her a comb and the heating pad. I said I would and got up to shower. Mildred soon called and I thanked her for looking after Mom and for keeping the house clean and organized. I arrived at the hospital by mid-morning. Mom was still very weak and her skin was yellow. At one point, she opened her eyes, and they appeared glowing yellow as well. I was taken aback at the sight, but tried not to show it. Mom told me that Dr. Whalen was looking for me. Just as she said that, he walked in. He's a younger doctor who was very engaging with Mom and I. He explained the procedure scheduled for today, and why it was necessary.

The doctor explained that the CT scan doesn't only show a tumor blockage of the bile duct to the small intestine, but also blood clots in her lungs that appeared to have come from her leg, hence the reason for the Heparin. They have her off all medications now since her system had to be empty to do the fluoroscopy. This is an imaging technique that uses x-rays to obtain real-time moving images of the internal structures of a patient through the use of a fluoroscope.

During this procedure, they would also insert a stent into the bile duct to get it to drain. Once the bile is able to drain into her intestine, then her bilirubin will increase and the jaundice will go away. Mom and I looked confused, scared and uncertain as to what all of this meant.

Dr. Whelan patiently explained to us that bilirubin is a reddish-yellow pigment found in bile that is produced by the breakdown of hemoglobin, a pigment in red blood cells. The liver removes bilirubin from the bloodstream and secretes it in the bile. Bile helps the body digest and absorb fatty foods. It also rids the body of certain waste products.

An excess of bilirubin in the blood can produce jaundice, a yellowish discoloration of the skin, the tissues, and the whites of the eyes. Jaundice is not a disease, but a symptom of various diseases. For example, jaundice may result if diseased liver cells fail to remove bilirubin from the blood. It may also occur if the common bile duct is blocked, preventing the secretion of bilirubin in the bile. Also, since Mom's bile was not passing out of her system, it has gotten into her blood, thus causing an infection.

The doctor explained that they were working diligently to get rid of this as well. Once all of these things were done, they would be able to consider and/or begin chemo. Mom said she might be up to two sessions of chemo, and Dr. Whelan said they could begin the first treatment here at Parkview once all these other problems are resolved.

Damn, that's a lot to take in. Mom was extremely thirsty, but we could not give her anything until after these procedures were done. Mom tried to sleep while we waited for them to come get her. She's so restless and physically weak. God, how it breaks my heart to see her like this.

The techs finally came to get us for the fluoroscopy. They took us to the first floor and had me sign the consent for the procedure. They kicked me out of the room after we got Mom on her belly. They told us she would be in "twilight" sedation and would not remember anything. Dr. Z was doing the procedure and would come out to see me in the waiting area once it was over. The time needed to perform the procedure would depend on whether they could get in the bile duct passageway.

At 2:45 p.m., Dr. Z approached me in the waiting area. He looked quite disturbed and drew me a picture of what they found. It appeared that a massive tumor had caused an obstruction between her stomach and the small intestine in the duodenum. This tumor was seeping blood, which was why Mom has been anemic and why she's having trouble with her bowels. Dr. Z said he has already contacted Dr. Whelan about this, as something needs to be done about this ASAP. They were able to get the stent in the bile duct to open it up, but because of the tumor, they cannot give her anymore Heparin, as it will keep bleeding. He wants to put a VT filter in her large artery to prevent any more clots from traveling to her lungs. They are taking her to the third floor to do that.

I just sat there, numb for what seemed like forever. I found myself running down the hall to call Linda, crying all the while explaining what the doctor had told me. I then called Hubby and left a message for Shirley and Mildred. I was starving, mad, upset, and felt I was losing my mind. God, how much more can you put my mother through?

I headed outside to drive off to *anywhere* until I realized I did not have the keys to the damn anteater-mobile! I stormed back inside and opted to go to the basement for something to eat. I had just placed a salad on my tray and was ordering fries when I heard a page over the intercom for *me*! That so freaked me out that I almost didn't hear the extension number I was to call.

Someone led me to a phone, and it turned out to be the folks in the Endoscopy department, where Mom was recovering. It was good that I didn't leave the hospital, because they needed me to come down to sign consents for the filter insertion. I grabbed my food and headed straight to the first floor, where I signed the consent. Mom was still sleeping off the twilight sedation, but they said they would be taking her to the third floor in a few moments.

Around 3:45 p.m., I met the team and the doctor who was going to insert the Vena Tech Vena Cava Filter into her main artery. He explained that they would make a quarter-inch incision into Mom's upper right thigh, through which they would insert a tube with an umbrella-like screen attached to the end. They would run this tube up her main artery and would open it up like an umbrella to stop any further blood clots from traveling up to her lungs, heart and brain. It should only take about fifteen minutes.

I stayed outside and tried to eat my salad – the fries were nasty – as I waited for Mom to come out. It was a short wait, because they soon wheeled Mom out to take her back to the room. The nurse said Mom now needs to lay flat on her back for the next four hours so the filter would adhere itself to the artery wall. Mom was knocked out, so that shouldn't be difficult. The nurse then told me that Dr. Whalen wanted to speak with me concerning what to do about the mass they found in her duodenum. He had left for the day, but would speak with me in the morning.

5:00 p.m.: The first hour of the vigil was not too bad, but soon Mom began to emerge from the haze and struggled to turn onto her side. I kept fussing with her to lie still on her back for the next four hours, but this became increasingly more difficult as the night drew on.

Nurse Beth had to come in every fifteen minutes to take her vitals, which made Mom even fussier. Every twenty minutes, Mom kept saying it was time to get out of this position, but we kept her on her back.

The last fifteen minutes were impossible. Mom was groggy and still in a haze, which made her think she could get up, take out her IV, and talk. She finally settled down at around 9:00 p.m., and the nurse said she could finally get on her side. Poor thing, she was so exhausted and uncomfortable on her back.

I watched Mom fall asleep and kissed her goodnight. She told me through her haze that I needed to get some sleep. Such a funny woman; even throughout all of this she still worries about me. God, I love her.

On the way home, I stopped at CVS and picked up, what else, junk food, as I was starving. Chips and dip anyone? I spoke with Hubby, who had gone to the kennel we had explored and said it seemed pretty decent for Zorro. I told him that after I spoke with Dr. Whalen in the morning I would let him know as to when I might need him to come here. I can't have him come here yet, as it will mean Mom is dead. I cannot face that possibility and must stay positive that this is all going to work out.

It was such a long day. I was up until 2:00 a.m., as it was too hard to sleep. I just kept seeing Mom's yellow, sad eyes looking at me.

Thursday, February 24th

I got up around 7:30 a.m. I had gone through Mom's bills last night and ran some errands to pay her overdue cable and water bills. Tonya called while I was in the shower, but I opted to call her later. I don't think I could stand another crying episode before I go see Mom. I made it to the hospital before 9:00 a.m., and the nurse was bathing Mom. She was still very weak and listless. Mom said Mildred had called, but I ran into Dr. Whalen while they were bathing her so we had our talk.

Dr. Whalen stated that the good news was that Mom's hemoglobin was up to 9.0. At this point, we have to build her up and get rid of the infection – reducing the bilirubin in her system – before we could begin any chemo. The bad news was that due to the position of this tumor in the wall of the duodenum, once the tumor shrinks, she could get a per-forated colon, which would be disastrous! This would mean they would have to go in to repair it, and he did not honestly believe she would survive it.

"How the hell is this good news?" I thought. I just stared at the doctor while he continued to tell me that if Mom's biliru-bin does not lower, they would not be able to do chemo at all. If that happens, Mom would have to be placed in hospice – either at home or in a facility. Knowing my mother like I do, I knew she would not want to be in a nursing home facility at all. I told him that even having anyone in her house would be hard for her to accept.

He said at this point we just need to wait and see how she responds and they would check her bilirubin daily, and know something for sure by Monday. I asked why didn't they see this tumor earlier when they did the first CT and MRI, and he said the liver mass might have occluded it. Getting more annoyed, I asked why they never noticed the blood in her stool and why they had kept telling me her dark stools had been caused from the iron. The doctor had no answer for that, but did say they would check her stool daily from here on. As for the bleeding or seeping of the tumor in her duo-denum, he said they would have to watch her and her stool, as they cannot go in to stop it.

I slowly made it back to Mom's room, where she rested. Her spa friend, Maxine, came by with flowers and another card. I filled her in as best I could so that she could tell her friends. Both Linda and Shirley stopped by, and while we sat quietly as Mom slept, I shared with them the current situation.

After they left, I decided to call Gordon and left him an un-hateful message about Mom's current status. I told him that, while I understood as per his last message he was going through something, I would be remiss if I did not fill him in on the severity of Mom's condition. I told him my call was to merely inform him of Mother's situation and he did not need to call me back. I did give him the number to the hospital and Mom's room number. I felt surprisingly subdued and calm.

Apparently, my call did hit a nerve. Gordon called Mom's room about two hours after I left that message. I answered the phone, recognized his voice, and passed the phone to Mom. We did not speak. Mom sounded weak, but spoke with him for a few minutes. From what I could make out from Mom's side of the conversation, he again said he would try to come visit her. *Whatever.* Mom and I did not talk about him after the call. She just slept.

Mom complained about being hot most of the day, but she did not have a temperature. She kept pushing the sheets off, and we placed cold compresses on her forehead. I hung out most of the day, and around 6:00 p.m., I went into one of the visitor's room to chill out. To my surprise, that room had a computer with free Internet access.

I had brought my laptop to work on stuff, and had planned to go to Kinko's later to finish our taxes. Instead, I was able to hang out in the room and finish them there. I told the nurses where I was and peeked in on Mom every few minutes. I left around 8:30 as Mom was sound asleep and looked peaceful.

Around 11:30 that night, Mom called me at the house. She said in a most playful, yet tired voice, *"So, you sneaked out on me, eh?"* I just laughed and told her she's the one that fell asleep on me. She told me they put a catheter in her and how much she hated that. Mom just loves to fuss.

Friday, February 25th
I arrived at the hospital around 10:00 a.m. and saw Dr. Whalen in the hallway. I asked about Mom's bilirubin count and he reported it had only dropped to 14.0. The normal count is 2.0, which is where she needs to be, or at least close to it, to begin chemo. He also ordered her to receive blood today, because her count dropped from 9.0 on Monday to 8.0 this morning.

Mom was half sleep when I walked in. She woke up while I was pulling the chair over and said, *"There's my sweet angel, how are you today?"* I leaned down, kissed her on her cheek, and told her I was fine. She said she ate some of her breakfast – some eggs and a bite of her toast. I told her that was great. She closed her eyes and dozed back off.

Soon, the nurse came in to give her blood – Mom is AB positive – and she's getting two bags this morning. They put a catheter in last night, as it was growing increasingly difficult to get her out of bed to the bathroom. Dr. Whalen was unsure how long they would have that in her, but Mom made it abundantly clear how much she hated it.

The more I sat and looked at her, the sadder I became; the internal bleeding and the potential loss of my mother was too much to bear today, for some reason. I left the room several times to cry. I called Seveda at one point and just broke down. Maybe because she's been so loving to me today, calling me her "angel", saying she loves me, that it just broke my heart to see such a strong woman so weak and helpless.

I stepped out into the hallway near the window and stared at the flat, gray horizon. I then made a call to Mrs. Grimes. She and her family were our childhood neighbors and great friends. Something compelled me to call her. She is such a positive and loving person and I knew she would want to know about Mom. I left a message and she soon called me back. I told her everything that was going on, and she said she and her hubby, Archie, would stop by if it was okay. I knew I had to tell Mom, which I did, and she was okay with them coming by as long as they were positive and not acting sad.

Mr. and Mrs. Grimes showed up that afternoon and visited for a few minutes. Mom and Archie have always been *"fuss-buddies"* and she tried to start in on him with jokes, but she was just too tired. I walked them out and got a salad across the street. They told me to come over for a home-cooked meal, but I told them I was not good company these days. They understood and told me they would stay in touch.

I got back up to the room after getting my salad to go, only to find Mom fast asleep. She ate pretty well at lunch - good for her that is. I hoped she would have an appetite for dinner. They brought her chicken noodle soup and the usual sherbet and fruit cup. She can't seem to tolerate too many solids right now.

She asked to drink an Ensure, which she finished. I gave her high praises and she just smiled. She also wanted to drink just the broth from the soup, so I put a straw in the bowl and she sucked down all the broth! *Way to go, Mom!* She touched my face as I wiped juice from her chin and told me that I was her, *"Precious angel"* and a *"Sweetie"*, and that she loved me. I tried not to cry even though her eyes were closed, and told her I loved her too.

I left around 7:00 that evening and finished our taxes in the small Wi-Fi room down the hall from her room. Hubby called while I was there, as he was heading out to see a play. I felt glad that he was getting out, as he's saddened about all of this as I am. I made it home around 8:00 and tried to watch Star Trek, but the damn phone kept ringing; mostly relatives from Oklahoma City wanting updates on Mom. I'm not sure how much Mom told them, so I just told the callers that she was tired and needed to have more tests run.

The next morning I got up later than usual. I had only fallen asleep around 3:30 a.m. I did a quick load of laundry, paid a bill, and arrived at the hospital around 10:00 a.m. Cousin Mildred was there with Mom and made it a point to tell me that she passed by the house and saw that Mom's van was still there – which is code for saying, *"Why hadn't you left the house yet?"* Mom's first words to me were, *"I thought you forgot about me…"* I frowned and thought, "*Great…thanks Mildred and shit, it was only 10:00, so mind your fucking business…and Mom, where's your son?* Okay, I needed to calm down…I took a deep breath, ignored Mildred, and told Mom I was sorry for being "late", but I had been doing a load of laundry and was trying to work on her taxes. Mildred repeated her drive-by observations, much to my annoyance. Finally, I laughingly replied to Mom, *"I see your spies are in place… good to know folks are watching out!"*

Mom said Dr. Whelan was looking for me, so I went to search for him – a good way to get away from Mildred. I spoke with him a few minutes later, and he told me Mom's blood count was up to 10, but her bilirubin had gone *up* to 15.0, which is not a good sign. This could mean either that the stent moved out of the duct, the duct was still blocked, or there were additional tumors we don't know about causing more damage.

He said we could go back in via the fluoroscope and see what's up and try to re-do it, or do one externally to drain the bile. Neither he nor I were comfortable with putting her through that, but I told him it would be up to Mom. I asked if she appeared to be getting better, and he said no, but to me, her eyes don't seem as yellow as they were on Wednesday.

I went back and told Mom what the doctor said, and explained what they wanted to do. She was not open to any of it, but did want to feel better. She's just so weak and tired! The nurse soon came in to give her an iron pill and some milk of magnesia to make her poop. As soon as she took it, she wanted to sit on the toilet. Mildred, the nurse, and I all helped Mom get to the bathroom, as she could not get there herself due to being so weak.

The nurse left and said she wanted Mom to sit up for about fifteen minutes, as it would be good for her. While Mom did poop a bit, she also began to feel nauseous and threw up. Her vomit was black and watery. I went to get the nurse, who got the aides to help clean Mom up and get her back into bed. Mom was so incredibly exhausted and tired from moving from the bathroom to the bed.

Mildred soon left and Mom fell back to sleep. Dr. Z came in after a while and said he may want to go back in to see what the problem was with the blockage. First, however, he wanted to order an ultrasound in the morning on her liver area, to see what the problem is. He's a bit of a fast-talking doctor who quickly came and left.

Mom does want to feel better, but are they just probing around? Do they really know what they're doing? My faith in them is rather shaky right about now, as Mom keeps growing weaker and weaker.

Mom tossed and turned most of the day, but did her best to sit up and eat her lunch. Shirley stopped by in the afternoon with a plant and candy in hand! She sat with us for a while and spoke to Mom when she was awake. Mom asked for pain meds later in the afternoon. Her back was bothering her despite the numerous back rubs I gave her. The nurse gave her morphine this time, as she really needed to get some sleep.

Shirley and I left after she dozed off. I followed her car to a soul-food place that served fried catfish filets. It was nice to get out while the sun was up and to get some home cooking. When I got home, I kept busy working on the bills, my laundry, and taxes. After I ate, I received calls from Mrs. Grimes and her son, my old childhood friend, Cliff. They gave Mom their love and told me they have her in their prayers. Hubby called around 11:00 p.m., my time, and we had a great conversation. I ended up staying awake until about 3:00 a.m. I wish I could fall asleep.

18

I'M RANTING LIKE CRAZY

February 27th through March 1st, 2005

I arrived at the hospital around 9:00 a.m. Mom was just returning from her ultrasound. She said she had met with Dr. Z, who told her they were going to go back in to re-do that endoscopy procedure. I asked where he was, and Nurse Rosemary said he had left, but Mom had already spoken with him. I firmly told her *I needed him to speak with me before going ahead, since I had to give consent.* She said she would page him. I hated to be such a pain, but I needed to know *why* this was necessary and ask what would he be doing differently this time. What was her bilirubin today? What happened to the stent he'd already put in? Did he screw it up?

Dr. Z soon called in, and I spoke with him. He indicated that Mom's bilirubin was *down* to 13.0, but it was not going down fast enough. The ultrasound showed the duct was dilated, but in order to be sure, and to see whether the stent had migrated up or down the duct, he would go back in through her mouth to see what's going on. He has her set up to do this at 11:00 tomorrow morning.

I asked him why this was a problem and he said it was not uncommon, as the stent is plastic and not sewn into the duct, but merely placed inside the duct. Mom had three large masses in her liver, and combined with the one in her duodenum, may be thwarting the stent's efficacy in draining the bile out of her gall bladder.

Dr. Whalen came into the room moments after I spoke with Dr. Z to check in on Mom. He clearly saw that I was upset with the entire circle of events. Truthfully, I had been in a shitty mood from the moment I got here. The crap about going back down her throat, the fucked-up, disrespectful way Nurse Rosemary nonchalantly said, *"This is what's going to happen,"* without the courtesy of giving me details about Mom's blood levels, the broken-down remote that I had to call service about, the fact that my mother is slowly dying, has me in a shitty mood! ...*Again, I digress...*

Dr. Whalen was kind and patient as always, even with me in this mood. He gently rubbed Mom's arm as he spoke with her about the need to go back down her throat for this second look.

I broke for a second and snapped, *"What happened the first time? Did Dr. Z make a mistake?"*

Mom gave me that "look" - you know - the one a parent gives when their child is acting out.

Dr. Whalen added, *"Your Mother wants to feel better and since this is the way to see what's going on...."*.

I interrupted, *"But can they promise to get it right this time?"* Mom shot me another look.

Dr. Whalen calmly replied that Dr. Z was the best upper GI doctor at the hospital, and that due to the extreme nature of Mom's masses, this type of problem was to be expected. I calmed down somewhat and asked if they could at least do this *on time* and as early as possible so that Mom didn't have to be uncomfortable for as long as she was last time.

After Dr. Whalen left, Mom opened her eyes wide and stared at me for what seemed like forever. After a few seconds, she told me to stop worrying about her. I just lost it and knelt on the floor, leaning as close to her face as I could. I told her no amount of her telling me *not* to worry, would ever make me not worry. She was my mother and I love her more than she could ever imagine.

Mom leaned into me, gently put her weak hand on my face and told me she knows I love her, but that I needed to have *faith* because her fate is in greater hands. I should not worry because she knows God is taking care of this. I told her I know, but I just don't trust these doctors because she's feeling worse. I kissed her and told her I would try to keep the faith. She wiped my tears as she did when I was a child and then laid back onto the bed.

Lunch soon came and Mom drank all her broth and ate some Jell-O. She then went back to sleep, so I went down to get a boring salad. Mrs. Grimes showed up about two hours later with flowers and a plate of food in tow. She and Mom visited for a while, and Mrs. Grimes told Mom about her own bout with colon cancer eight years ago. After she left, I massaged Mom's back with some eucalyptus oil, which she always enjoys. It was a pretty weepy day today, and I was so exhausted that I left mom around 6:00 that evening when the nurse came in to give her a pain pill so that she could rest for tomorrow's endoscopy.

Back at the house, I spoke with Linda, Hubby, and Tonya at length. Hubby and I "watched" the Oscar's together – it was great seeing both Morgan Freeman and Jamie Foxx win. I made myself go to bed by midnight and set the TV timer for one hour. I think I fell asleep before the TV went off.

Monday, February 28th

I got up at 7:00 a.m. so that I could head out to the Medicaid office for Aunt Mable's certification. I was able to get a copy of the Power of Attorney form Mom had given them for Auntie. Mom did not have a copy and I needed one since I am the backup agent for Mom in regards to Aunt Mable's care. They needed me to contact my Aunt's pension folks to get the info on how much life insurance they have on her so they can determine her assets for eligibility. The caseworker, David, gave me their phone number and his fax so I can get them to forward the info to them. What a pain...

I arrived at the hospital by 9:00, and found the aides bathing Mom. I oiled her legs and back and then we waited for them to take her down for the endoscopy. I saw Dr. Carr down the hall, but he has yet to come into the room. About an hour later, I turned Mom to oil her left side, and to my horror, found two one-inch plastic tubes pressed into her left hip and buttock, leaving indentations! I removed the one from her hip and found a quarter-inch depression in her skin from the damn tube! I went off and buzzed for the nurse, simple-assed Rosemary, to come in.

She was not available, but the aide came in and saw the tubes – the one I had moved, the skin indentations, and the tube still leaving an imprint - in her buttock. I removed that one as well and she asked to look at them. She said they were respiration tubes that had apparently been left in the bed. I started yelling now. How could these pieces been left so haphazardly in her bed for her to lie on? The aide had no answers and hurried to find out. She took the tubes with her. I should have kept them for evidence, but I found others on the floor. The aide came back in a few minutes later and said she told the director about it. The director would follow up and find out why and how this had happened. *What the fuck?*

They finally came up to get Mom for the procedure at 12:15 – this is one *slow-assed* place. Dr. Clark was doing the procedure today, and according to the smart-assed tech, they would be removing the stent from last week and putting in a new one. No one knows why this one was acting up. It may be clogged, or it may have migrated.

About five minutes after they took her out of the room, Dr. Clark came to discuss Mom. He showed me her internal photo from last week and showed me her chart levels. As it turns out, *he did not feel they needed to re-do the procedure today, because her levels were still dropping!* I was shown the bilirubin progression since they put the stent in on Wednesday: Thursday – 16.7, Friday – 14.8, Saturday – 15.1, Sunday – 13.8 and today – 11.5. Dr. Clark stated that while he understood Dr. Z's concern about that slight increase, he did not agree that it was critical to go in and do this procedure again.

He wanted to continue to watch the numbers and have her on NPO (nothing by mouth) after midnight again, just in case they have to do the procedure tomorrow. Looking at her film, the stent looked like it should continue to drain well, but the blockage was so tight it might be difficult to put another one in if we take this one out.

Well, damn! Finally, someone with some sense! I thanked Dr. Clark and they decided that Mom could be taken back to her room. We would have had to wait, due to their being short-staffed, but I guess since the male smart-assed tech felt bad about being a *smart-ass,* he volunteered to bring Mom back up. I did thank him and his assistant, and we got Mom back in bed. The nursing staff was overly pleasant and attentive, and got everything Mom asked for – more broth, an Ensure, and some fresh water. Guess I need to go off more often!

Mom was pretty drowsy for the rest of the day, but she drank half of her Ensure shake and some water. She did not drink her broth, and fell asleep quickly.

The next day, I finally got through to Aunt Mable's retirement agency in Washington D.C. about what type of life insurance she had, so I could inform the Medicaid people. The caseworker there was really great and said she would fax the type of insurance policy to David at Medicaid.

It snowed overnight – about two inches – so I swept off the steps, the sidewalk and the car, and then headed to Denny's to get an omelet to take to the hospital.

I saw Dr. Carr and his nurse, Mary, as I was heading to Mom's room. They stopped to speak and said he was glad the bilirubin was going down. It's now 9.9 and he has Mom scheduled for a scan of her gall bladder today to see what's going on. They planned to insert a PICC line (Peripherally Inserted Central Catheter) in her arm so they don't have to keep changing IV sites every three days. Nice. Finally! Some good news.

I made it to Mom's room to find the IV nurse already there to explain the PICC procedure to Mom. The nurse told me about the scan and that Mom had been NPO since midnight. So, of course, Mom was cranky and dry and requesting fluids. They said they would be taking her in in less than two hours...*ugh!* After which she would be able to eat and drink. The PICC was going to go into her upper left arm, as it's deeply inserted into her large artery so all draws and injections can go in this portal. The nurse was very gentle and completed the process quickly.

They then took Mom down for the scan, which lasted about two hours. When she came back, she was so thirsty that I immediately gave her some Ensure. While I was giving it to her, the aide came in and whispered to me that Mom was still NPO, as they had not been able to finish the procedure. *Fuck that shit.* I told her Mom was extremely thirsty and they would just have to do it again *tomorrow.* She delivered the message to Nurse Mary, who came in to face "the beast" in me. She is mad cool though, and was okay with my choice to not starve my mother anymore.

As it turns out, they came back up around 3:30 that afternoon, citing they were going to finish the procedure even though Mom had ingested fluids. Mom said she would do it only if she did not have to wait around because that gurney was SO uncomfortable. The tech said there was no one else downstairs and she would go right in and out. I went with her this time and the turnaround was fast; we got back up into the room in no time.

I did my best to make Mom as comfortable as I could. She asked for a pain pill and soon fell asleep. I kissed her goodbye and told her I loved her. She woke up from her haze and told me she loved me too, and to drive safely.

I drove around and ended up at the Scott's grocery store in Georgetown Square in search for some vegetable lasagna. I found it and some pineapple juice for mom. On my way out, I noticed the theatre sign in the mini-mall area and saw that *The Incredibles* was playing. Seveda and I were just talking about me going to see something funny, and I had mentioned wanting to see this movie!

I did a drive-by the box office and saw this was a second-run *dollar* house and my movie would begin in ten minutes, at 7:00 p.m. Coincidence? I think not. God was at work here. I debated for a minute and decided to not test fate. The movie was really funny, and I got home before 9:00. I gave Shirley a call, and she helped me get centered again and kept me from eating everything in the house.

I also chatted with Hubby earlier in the day and made his airline reservation – he'll be here next Tuesday evening. I'm so glad he is coming, but also fearful that his coming marks the end of my mother.

19

THE HARD TRUTH

March 2nd through March 5th, 2005

The next morning, I saw Dr. Carr first thing when I arrived at the hospital and he told me that Mom's bilirubin count was down to 8.7. However, he bluntly but gently informed me that Mom's cancer had spread so much throughout her system that he did not believe her bilirubin count would ever be low enough to get the chemo. Even if it did, he does not believe she would be strong enough to endure it. Instead, he wanted us to focus on making her as comfortable as possible.

He also wanted us to consider doing another endoscopy procedure to insert a bigger and longer stent. While the one in her now is working, it wasn't working as fast as he would like. He told me that a larger stent may or may not make a difference in her liver acid count, which has been going up consistently for the past week, but if it did work, Mom would feel a bit more comfortable.

"What do I have to lose?" Mom said when asked if she wanted to try going through it again. The doctor arranged to come for her around 1:00 that afternoon for the procedure.

On another note, Dr. Carr said we needed to think about the big picture with Mom and her health. He didn't feel she could go back home and suggested we consider hospice care at this point. I asked Mom what she thought and asked if she wanted to go home.

"What would I be able to do there?" she asked, as if she knew she needed assistance. I began to cry, and Dr. Carr stepped back and let us have our moment.

I leaned closer to Mom, began rubbing her back, and again quietly asked her what she wanted. Did she want to try hospice as Dr. Carr explained? Mom opened her eyes and said *"Why not?"*

Dr. Carr indicated he would inform the proper department. Mom was really wiped out and ready to sleep. I oiled her back and feet and helped her turn on her right side, and she slept until the gurney came down to get her for the procedure.

Down in the endoscopy room that same smart-assed tech was there trying to be somebody's friend, but not really; you know, "fake" nice? We waited forty-five minutes for the doctor to arrive, and Mom was not pleased, as the gurney was extremely uncomfortable. She fussed and fussed. Honestly, I enjoyed hearing her fuss; it made her sound full of life. I asked the doctor if her having her breakfast this morning would interfere with them doing the test and he said no.

They finally rolled her in and I waited out in the hallway, staring out the window at the gray skyline.

Now we *wait*. While I waited, Tonya came by. She had gone up to Mom's room and the nurse told her where we were. It was nice sitting with her without the girls, as it gave us a chance to really talk. I went to get us a cup of fattening white mocha coffee, and when I returned, I found Tonya sitting with Mom's friend, Maxine, from her spa. She had also gone up to the room and had been directed to where we were waiting.

The doctor had also stopped by to speak with me. I turned around and there he was, just a few feet away, talking on his cell phone. When he finished, he came back and told us that the procedure had gone well and they were able to put in a bigger, longer stent. Mom should be back upstairs in a few minutes. Maxine didn't want to stay for long, but did want to see her.

We walked back to the exam area, where they were getting Mom ready to go back to her room. The tech-jerk was annoyed that all of us were down in his turf, but Maxine just walked past him and looked at Mom for a second. We all then walked out. Maxine left and Tonya and I went upstairs, and the staff made it upstairs with Mom by the time we got there. We kept ourselves busy getting her settled back in her bed. Mom was knocked out and would be so for some time.

Tonya stayed only a few minutes longer and then left, but Shirley came by shortly afterward and sat with us while Mom continued to sleep. She read scriptures to Mom and brought some fresh carrot/parsley juice with her for mom to drink later. Nurse Mary, my favorite, was on call for the evening and said that Mom was back on NPO because the procedure had irritated her pancreas and her ingesting anything would run her at risk for an infection. She should be better in the morning.

Dr. Carr happened by and spoke about hospice again. He said he would be sending a nurse over to speak to us with more details tomorrow. Dr. Carr said they would want to know if Mom would be alone at home. I told him that I would be staying with her, and he mentioned that we could get a nurse in the home daily if I wanted it.

Dr. Carr then spoke the dreaded words I wasn't ready to hear. *"At the rate of your mother's deterioration I only expect her to be with us for only two more weeks."* Hard news to hear, but he felt he needed to share his thoughts with us. I know Mom is a tough bird and will fight to stay with us as long as she is able. *Shit,* as stubborn as Mom is, I always knew she would outlive us *all.* Hell, but what *do* doctors know? Her faith is strong; I wanted to believe she can beat this!

I swelled up inside and for the first time understood the rage my father felt when the doctors asked him to choose to save my mother or my unborn brother when she was in labor those many years ago.

I couldn't breathe, I couldn't speak. I was mad...mad at everything and at God. How could He do this to her? Her faith was so strong and she did not deserve this.

Mom looked so peaceful sleeping, but as the drugs wore off, she grew fitful and restless. I only want peace for her. I called Linda and Gregor after Shirley and I left and told them what Dr. Carr said. Suddenly, I went into task mode again. I thought I should go to the funeral home and plan for Mom, and Linda said she would go with me.

Thursday, March 3rd

Dr. Carr was front and center when I arrived at the hospital the next morning. Mom was much more alert than she's been all week. We chatted for a while, mostly about how she wants to *"Pass a turd." Nice, Mom…*She's so eloquent. Nurse Krista had given her a suppository but it wasn't doing anything. Mom got on the bedpan twice, but only passed gas. Krista said they might give her a fleet enema if this does not work.

Dr. Carr said her bilirubin was down to 7.4 and that the new stent was doing well, as her liver acids were also going down. Soon Janet, the hospital social worker, came in to talk about hospice. She went into detail about the Hospice House, located out west of Fort Wayne near Linda's house. She explained the place was professionally staffed and designed to make every patient comfortable. The rooms were private, with facilities for family members to spend the night.

Mom could also opt to have hospice in her home with a nurse and aide coming in daily for a few hours. The hospital would also be just a phone call away in the event we needed them. Mom mulled over both options, but did not make a choice. Janet said she would check and see if Hospice House had a bed available, and would get back with us.

After Janet left, I asked Mom what she wanted to do. Mom said she would hate to have me drive all the way out there every day. I told her that the drive was no big deal, and that it was closer to Linda. Plus, I could stay with her there as well and she would get more individualized care. I only talked it up because Mom seemed to be leaning toward the Hospice House. Janet came back a few minutes later and told us the facility did have a bed available. Mom was on the bedpan and not able to give an answer, and Janet said she would return in a half-hour.

After Mom finished and got comfortable, I asked her again what she wanted to do. She just looked at me and said she might feel better at the Hospice House. She didn't look sad, just frustrated. At no point has Mom cried or looked defeated during this journey. All she keeps harping on is how it's affecting me – my money, my job, my husband. She just doesn't get it…there is nothing I wouldn't do for her; and there is no one more important than *her*.

The nurse ended up giving Mom a fleet enema so she could have a bowel movement, which worked big time. They had to change her bedding twice. Linda and Mildred arrived while Dawn, from Hospice House, came to speak with me about their facility. I had Linda sit with us as she described the place and their services. It sounded like a great place and I planned on going by the facility tonight to check it out. They would be able to take Mom as soon as tomorrow.

When I got back to Mom's room, Mildred was feeding Mom Jell-O. I explained everything to Mom and asked if she wanted to speak with Dawn. She said no, and told me to handle it. Linda and Mildred soon left, and Mom was still pooping from the enema. We watched television and I hung out until about 5:00 that evening. I told Mom I was going to check out Hospice House and would be back in the morning. I told Mom I loved her and would see her tomorrow.

I took the long drive to Hospice House and found it easily. The facility was clean, looked new, and the staff there was very nice. Mom would have her own room in the eleven-bed facility. Nurse Ruth Ann explained how Mom's "final days" would be, and how they are here to not only help Mom be comfortable, but to help the family be comfortable. The woman made me cry, but I felt good about this place.

When I got back out to the van, I began crying uncontrollably again. I couldn't stop. Finally, I was able to call Gregor, who thought Mom had passed since I was crying so hard and couldn't speak. I told him she was still with us but I had just left the hospice facility and could not stop crying.

Hubby kept telling me he loved me and that Mom loved me and how everything would be all right. I calmed down after speaking with him and drove home.

20

THE MOVE TO HOSPICE HOUSE

March 4ᵗʰ, 2005

I woke up around 6:00 a.m. and started my day. I told myself, *"No crying today, dammit!"* as I dropped off some bills and got to the hospital by 8:30. Mom was half-asleep, but greeted me with the usual, *"Hi Princess."* I began to rub her back with some eucalyptus oil when I noticed blood on the pad by her behind. I thought she was bleeding from her anus, but Nurse Rosemary didn't think so. She wiped her and noted it was coming from her vaginal area. The nurse explained that in situations like Mom's, the cancer might now be present in her cervical area. Damn, I thought…what more does my mother have to endure?

A few minutes later, Pam, the nurse's aide, came by, ready to wash Mom. Pam had been so loving toward Mom during her stay and she always greeted Mom with a big hug. Mom hugged her back and we told her we wanted her to have the plant and flowers Mom received during her hospital stay. Pam was appreciative and gave me a hug as well.

Dr. Carr's nurse, Mary, also came by to say goodbye right when the Ambulette guys came to transport Mom to the hospice facility. I called Linda, Shirley, and Mildred, and told them of the move. I met up with Shirley at the house and we rode out there together. By the time we got there, the van had already arrived and staff was getting Mom settled in. The nurse who gave me the tour the previous evening was the same one who gave the orientation today. Ruth Ann is an amazing individual who talked and walked us through their process and procedures. She took off Mom's IV from Parkview and gave her 10mg morphine and 0.5mg of Ativan to make her relax. It wore off by 12:30, so they gave her another 15mg of morphine, as she was still quite uncomfortable and in a lot of pain.

Mildred showed up and sat with Mom while Shirley and I left briefly to get a bite to eat. I called Linda, Maxine, and Gordon and told them where she was and the facility's phone number. When it came to Gordon, I ended up leaving a message, as usual.

Shirley hung out with me until 6:00 that evening. I told her I would take her back to her car and then pick up my coat from the cleaners. It's supposed to snow AGAIN tonight. I made it back to Hospice House and spent the evening with Mom. I did plan to spend the night and told Greg and Linda I was doing so. However, around 10:30 that evening, I realized I had not brought along my blood pressure meds, had nothing to sleep in, and my cramps were kicking my ass.

Mom was sound asleep and it had started to snow. I left the facility at 11:00 and went back to the house where I packed up some food, a tee shirt and went to bed.

The next morning, I got up before 6:00 a.m. and was back at the hospice within an hour. Mom was just waking up. *"Are you coming or going?"* she asked. I smiled and told her I was coming in for the day. I told her about the snow (wet and slushy) and described how nice this facility was. Mom said she felt really rested and peaceful. I gave her some water, but it was room temp, so I went to the kitchen to get some fresh water and ice. Upon my return, I asked Mom if she was hungry.

"What do you have?" she asked. I told her this place was stocked with whatever she wanted. She could not give me a preference, so I went and got her some oatmeal, diced peaches, milk and apple juice. She only managed to drink the juice before she grew tired and soon fell back to sleep.

I curled up in the recliner and took a nap too. At 9:00 a.m., the aide came in to apply a topical pain gel on Mom's left hip, and then gave her a pill to help her relax. We turned her over to her right side and I noticed more blood between her legs and a bruise on her pubic area. The aide got some warm washcloths and we cleaned between her legs. It appears the blood was still coming from her vaginal area. It's not coming from the anus or catheter. After we finished, Mom went to sleep but Dr. Smitt came in to explain that perhaps she has yet another tumor in her uterus that was bleeding. That's just what the folks at Parkview said. How I hoped they were wrong. Damn...

Linda called later in the morning. She had made an appointment for us to meet with Juanita Ellis at Ellis Funeral home the following morning at 11:00. She would meet me there. I called Shirley and asked her to sit with Mom while I go to Ellis'; she said she'd be here by 10:00. I then called Mrs. Grimes and told her that I would not be going out to her function tonight. I was too exhausted, had nothing to wear, and honestly did not feel too sociable. She said she understood, and would come by tomorrow with some dinner for me. I told her she did not have to, but she lovingly told me to hush and allow someone to take care of *me* for a change.

They kept Mom on the 15mg of morphine and 0.5mg of Ativan. It seems to work well with her level of discomfort, so she now gets doses at 9:00 a.m., 5:00 p.m. and then again at 11:00 p.m. Mom rested most of the day. This place is really nice and they go out of their way to make us all comfortable. I stayed until midnight, and then left her sleeping. At the house, I started a load of laundry and went to bed with the clothes in the dryer.

Sunday, March 6th
I woke up abruptly at 7:30. I felt as if I overslept and was in full panic-mode. I quickly finished drying the laundry and washed up, making it to Mom before 8:30, only to discover that she was not yet awake. She had not received any meds since the night before, as she had yet to wake up for water or food.

She was like this for most of the day, only opening her eyes long enough for me to ask if she was hungry or thirsty. Each time I asked her, she would only nod, shake her head, or moan "yes" or "no". I've not seen her this weak, and the nurses told me these were signs of her body shutting down. *Damn...*

Shirley came by on time and said she would read to Mom from the Bible while I was gone. She brought along a plate of food Mildred had made for Mom. I soon left and met Linda at Ellis's Funeral home. The funeral home was literally a few blocks down the street from Mom's place, and one of the few black-owned funeral homes in Fort Wayne. This funeral home had performed the service for our oldest brother, Cletus and for our father, years earlier. *"Hmm, maybe they'll give us a discount since we've given them so much business..."* I thought, inappropriately.

Mrs. Ellis was very solemn, respectful and sad to hear about my mother, as she's known Opal Jean for many years. She sat us down to go through their "menu" of packages. I explained Mom was quite specific about wanting to be cremated, so she gave me all the info for their cremation packages and a selection of urns. The whole business was like buying a car...it was so surreal.

Stupid, inappropriate thoughts kept creeping into my head, so much so that I could not help but to laugh. Not just a little bit, but full, out-loud laughing. It was so inappropriate, but I couldn't help myself. I mean silly, goofy, laughter. I apologized to Mrs. Ellis and made the excuse that I laugh when I get nervous. Damn... what the hell is wrong with me? I know Linda thought I was having a breakdown.

Linda and I went for salads after that experience, and when we returned to Hospice House, Mom was still asleep. Shirley said she was given pain meds at 11:30, and she had swabbed her mouth with a small sponge on a stick since she would not take any water. I let Mom know I was back but she only managed to mutter, *"Uh-huh"*.

Linda and Shirley left soon thereafter and I got a call from Hubby. I shared with him the events of the day and my not-so-appropriate behavior at the funeral home. Hubby's been amazingly supportive and strong throughout all of this, and we're both eager to see each other.

Mom continued to sleep all afternoon. A few of her swim buddies came by with more flowers and stayed awhile and shared stories, laughed, and watched Mom sleep. Mrs. Grimes and her son, Claude, came by a bit later and dropped off dinner for us. She is such a sweet lady, though Claude appeared as if he wished he were anywhere but here. I don't blame him. After they left I put in one of the many Clint Eastwood movies for Mom to listen to while she slept. I figured she would like waking up and seeing "Mr. Cool."

A few hours passed and Mom still had not fully awakened. She muttered when you got close to her face, but she would not eat or drink. The evening nurse explained that Mom's body is shutting down, but she is not in discomfort.

At 11:00, I decided to spend the night. I moved the sleeper chair to the other side of the room by the window and moved the dining table and chairs by the door. The staff got me sheets, and before going to bed, Mom woke up briefly. I asked if she wanted water and she nodded. She was unable to draw through the straw so I had the nurse bring me ice. I put a small cube in her mouth.

Mom appeared to be in such discomfort so I told the nurse, who said it was time for her evening meds. They gave them to Mom via an oral syringe. I tucked Mom in and we both turned in for the night.

Monday, March 7th

I woke up around 4:30 a.m. to use the bathroom. Mom slept soundly and had done so through the night as per the nurse. She was also pretty unresponsive throughout the morning. I put in another Eastwood video and held her hand while she slept. I also rubbed oil on her back and side after she was cleaned and changed.

The staff came in every two hours to turn her so that Mom would not develop bedsores. Dr. Smitt came by late in the morning to speak with me, indicating that Mom was failing and growing progressively worse. Hearing that upset me so much that I decided to go to see Aunt Mable and tell her the truth about Mom. I contacted Linda and asked her to come by to watch Mom while I went to the nursing home to pick up Auntie. I shared with Linda what the doctor had said and then I called Mildred, who would try to stop by today as well.

Linda got to the hospice facility by 11:30, and I sped out to Aunt Mable's. When I got there, I found out that the director, Janet, had already told her about Mom. She was very sorry to hear about Mom and helped me get Aunt Mable. Unfortunately, Aunt Mable was on an outing with a group of others from the center, but I only had to wait about ten minutes before she showed up. After they got her off the van, I pulled her to the side.

I greeted her warmly. At first, she smiled at me, but then her expression changed, replaced by a look of horror. *"Opal's dead, isn't she?"* she cried. I told her no; of course not, but I did tell her that Mom was really sick. I explained that she had broken her hip because she has cancer in her bones, liver, and lungs. Aunt Mable began crying uncontrollably, and so did I. I embraced her and we just held each other and cried for several minutes. I told her Mom was hanging in there and asked if she wanted to see her. She said yes so fast that she attempted to turn her wheelchair around to head out to the van. I helped her outside and Janet helped us get her in the van.

We made good time back to Hospice House. Once she saw Mom, Aunt Mable began crying immediately. I just hugged her shoulder and cried with her. She grasped Mom's hand, sat next to her, and told her how everything is in God's hand and how he will get her back on her feet soon. It just broke my heart to see Aunt Mable and Mom together in this situation.

Linda, Mildred, and I were all a mess, crying and carrying on. Mom did try to open her eyes a bit, but she was pretty non-responsive, vocally. Her breathing was labored, and at times, her exhalations sounded like vocal responses to Aunt Mable's questions. Auntie teased Mom about how she now had to put up with her fussing at her and dared her to wake up and fuss her back. She stayed and visited for about two hours, and kissed Mom several times while she slept.

I asked Aunt Mable if she wanted to come back tomorrow and she said, *"yes"* before I could finish the question. Aunt Mable chose when to end the visit, citing she wanted Mom to get some rest. During our drive back to the nursing home, Aunt Mable kept repeating: *"God's will be done..."* for Mom. It was a very emotional visit, but I'm glad it took place.

After dropping off Aunt Mable, I was able to go by Mom's house and take a quick shower before heading back to Hospice House. Mildred was going to stay with Mom until 4:00, and so I grabbed some food and a change of clothes before heading back.

It was past 4:00 p.m. when I returned, and Mildred had already left. Soon, Shirley came by and hung out with us until about 7:00. Tonya came by later and we hung out until 9:30 while we sat and talked with Mom. She opened her eyes a little bit, but for the most part, she kept her eyes shut.

During the time Shirley was there, Mom had difficulty breathing to the point we thought this was the end for her. She was trying to cough, but could not catch her breath to do so. She opened up her eyes and looked up toward the ceiling, then reached up toward the ceiling and held her breath. I felt so helpless and could only tell her it was okay to let go, to not fight it. I told her that Aunt Mable, Gordon, and I would be all right and it was okay to let go. Mom then relaxed her arms, closed her eyes and fell back to sleep. We called the nurse for more meds, which they gave her, and she continued to sleep until I went to bed.

Tuesday, March 8th

Mom continued her heavy, labored breathing all night. Morning came, but not once did she open her eyes to look at us all day throughout the day. She was unable to take in any fluids, and her urine count was only 25cc. She's failing and there's nothing I can do about it. I made one last-ditch effort to contact Gordon. This time, I found his email address at his job on the OSU website and sent a note to him there as well as to his regular Yahoo account.

Shirley came by at 10:30 that morning, and I went to pick up Aunt Mable. She was at an appointment with the cardiologist to check her pacemaker, and I waited around and went for a short ride to my old high school, located just down the street. When I got back, Auntie had returned. She wanted to eat her lunch there before leaving, so I waited with her in the dining area. *Good Lord, the staff here is sooo slow.* It seemed to take twenty minutes to pass out water, coffee, and trays of food to about twenty people, with only one unmotivated person doing it. Could they be any slower? An hour and a half later, we left for Hospice House. *Patience, Nat, patience...*

Aunt Mable was less teary today and determined to get Mom back on her feet. Mildred was also in the room with Shirley when we arrived. Aunt Mable asked Mildred if Mom had gotten up today. That just broke our hearts, but was also precious to watch at the same time. The two sisters visited, with Aunt Mable taking on the role as the older, "fussing" sister, and Mom taking on the role as the "baby" sister.

For the first time all day, Mom did utter some sounds, more like grunts or moans. She was overdue for her pain meds, as her last dose had been at 3:30 a.m. Aunt Mable said to go ahead and give her something, as I had asked the staff to hold off medicating her again until they had their visit. Mom had not appeared to be in any kind of distress until now. Meds were given - 15mg Morphine/0.5mg Ativan, at 1:50 that afternoon.

Aunt Mable was soon ready to go, and I took her back to the nursing home. Mildred said she would stay with Mom until I returned. Shirley was leaving, but would be back around 5:00 p.m. so I could go pick up Gregor from the airport. I dropped off Aunt Mable at the nursing home and told her I would be back tomorrow to pick her up for another visit.

It was cold outside and trying to snow again! Gregor is just going to *love* this. When I got back to Hospice House, Mildred was ready to go. I sat with Mom until Shirley came back around 5:00. Hubby called about 5:20 to let me know he was at O'Hare airport in Chicago, and his flight would be delayed due to high winds there. I left anyway to fill up on gas and to get to the airport just in case his flight arrived on time.

Hubby's flight arrived, safe and sound and not too late. It sure was great seeing him. He was surprised at how *cold* it was here and at the amount of snow on the ground. We went to grab dinner at a nearby restaurant and brought it back to Hospice House. Shirley was still there with Karen, an old friend from our former church, Shepherd of the City. Karen looked the same and greeted me with a hug. She said the church was aware of Mom's condition and had been praying for her. Both Shirley and Karen left soon after we arrived.

Gregor was startled at Mom's appearance, and at first was unsure what to do. I held his hand and told him to just sit beside her and talk to her about what's going on in his life. Mom did not open her eyes, but she did her best to let out a quiet moan. Hubby did his best to settle in with everything. I had warned him beforehand how she would appear, but I could tell he was a bit overwhelmed by everything. Still, he hung in there. I put in a Carol Burnett video for Mom to listen to and to help lighten the mood while Hubby spoke with her. He tried to get comfortable in the recliner, but opted to sleep on the foldout chair.

Mom was extremely restless the entire night. Her level of pain seemed to jump, especially when the evening aide crew came in to turn her at 10:30 p.m. They appeared really rough with her, to my displeasure. I know they didn't mean any harm, but I told the nurse after they left that I did not want Mom turned anymore, as it was too uncomfortable for her.

I explained that they caused Mom to yelp out in pain and her eyes would open but not focus on anything. It was too horrible to put her through every two hours. The nurse said that she understood and everything would be all right. I also asked her to give Mom more pain meds, as her last dose was at 11:50 p.m.

Hubby was in deep snore-mode, a familiar sound that was refreshing to hear. Mom's breathing grew more belabored, so the nurse came in at 4:00 a.m. and gave her a 20mg dosage of morphine. She said she had been informed that I did not want Mom turned, but she wanted to see if we could turn her thirty minutes after she had her meds; perhaps it would not be as painful for her. I told her okay and at 4:45, she came back in to turn Mom on her side.

Mom still yelped out and was so uncomfortable I asked them to stop. The nurse said we should probably give her something for pain every three hours, and that she also had something for her upper respiratory congestion. She placed about four drops of some medicine under her tongue that was supposed to help relieve congestion. Unfortunately, Mom continued to have breathing problems, coughing, and sounds of snoring for the remainder of the morning. I lowered the head of her bed a bit, and by 6:00 a.m. she seemed to not sound in as much distress. I rubbed her arms, head and legs with oil and spoke softly to her, but it did not seem to do much good. *God, please give her some peace.*

21

ONE LONG NIGHT, ONE LAST BREATH...

Wednesday, March 9ᵗʰ, 2005

This has been one long night. I have such a headache and Gregor and I got little sleep. He was finally able to get back to sleep, but I'm now restless and tired. I keep watching Mom's chest to make sure she's breathing. Of course, that's only when she's not coughing or making those horrible guttural sounds in her efforts to breathe. I think I'll wait until this afternoon to get Aunt Mable. Perhaps Gregor will want me to drop him off at Mom's house so he can wash up and change.

The nurse and an aide came in at 7:30 a.m. to turn her – I promptly told them no, not now. I'll have them give her the meds in about an hour and then at 9:00, we can try to put her back on her back if she does not appear to be in too much distress. Shirley came by around 12:30 so that Gregor and I could go get him some sweat pants and then pick up Aunt Mable.

Auntie was so happy to see Gregor, and eager to go see Mom. When we got to Hospice House, Mom was still in distress, though breathing a bit better. Shirley said around 2:30 Nurse Dave had increased her pain meds to 30mg and then they turned Mom on her back.

We had a real nice visit. Aunt Mable, Shirley, Linda, Gregor and I reminisced, laughed, and cried about our lives and how Mom made life fun. While holding Mom's hand, Aunt Mable would smile and speak to her. *"You hear us talking about you, Opal Jean?"* It was bittersweet. We had also popped an Eastwood film into the VCR and we described the scenes to Mom since she was not opening her eyes.

Gregor and I took Aunt Mable back to the nursing home and then went to the house to shower and deal with bills. When we got back to Hospice House, Linda and Shirley were still visiting. Mom continued to have breathing problems and the staff is now giving her pain meds every hour. Linda told me she had spoken with her daughter, who indicated she was going to find Gordon and see why he was not here. Her daughter was also in Columbus, Ohio, attending school. While we were talking, Linda's daughter called back and said she had found Gordon and his wife, Monica, at their home. She said she had spoken with Gordon at length.

Reportedly, Gordon said he knew Mom's situation and had received all of our messages. He said he would probably be in Fort Wayne this weekend. Apparently, Gordon was made aware that Mom was critical, was given the phone number of Hospice House, and was told that he should call and have us put the phone to his mother's ear and talk to her before it was too late. I told Linda to thank my niece for her attempt. Whatever Gordon was going through must be major for him not to be here. I hold no ill will toward my brother; life is too short.

After Linda and Shirley left, Gregor and I settled in for the evening. I pulled my chair up next to Mom. We watched TV and I rubbed her hand with oil. Around 11:00 p.m., the nurse came in to give Mom another dose of meds. She and her aides were very kind, gentle and sensitive to Mom's pain, and worked with me to keep her comfortable.

I continued to sit with Mom, my hand on hers. Gregor alerted me that Mom was opening her eyes. I looked and found her eyes open, but not focused. They began to open even wider as her breathing grew more labored. Her eyes then rolled back into her head and I knew the end was near. I could not look at her with her eyes like that, but I held on tightly to her and told her it was okay to let go. She took one deep breath and held it for what seemed like forever.

I could still feel the pulse beating in her hand and Gregor said her chest was still moving, but her eyes were now closing. I braved one last look at her, and as she grabbed that one last breath, I told her that I loved her. Gregor stood beside me, holding me as I held Mom's hand. I continued to feel her pulse until it stopped. She was gone... she was gone. It was 11:25 p.m.

Greg held me while I cried uncontrollably. We sat for about five minutes, and then I buzzed for the nurse to come in. They gave us plenty of respect and time to say our goodbyes. I called Linda and Shirley and they made their way over quickly. I then called Mildred and Mrs. Grimes. I asked Gregor to leave a message for Gordon, which he did. I then called and left a message for Tonya. Gordon called back and I had Gregor talk with him. Gordon asked Gregor how I was and then explained that he'd been going through some deep stuff himself. Gregor asked if he could let him in on what was going on, and Gordon said he would call back tomorrow.

Linda arrived first and gave me a hug. She sat with Mom and I told her how peaceful she went. Shirley came next and knelt down beside the bed and kissed her hand. We then hugged. The nurse came back in and told us she called Ellis to come get Mom in about two hours. They told us to take our time, but to not forget our things. We all sat for a while and then packed everything up.

I kissed Mom goodbye for the last time, my tears falling on her face. She couldn't wipe them away this time. This time, I'm left alone to wipe them myself. I stood there sobbing, staring at her, unable to leave. I didn't want to leave her alone. Gregor embraced me while helping me realize that she had already left, and would not be alone or in pain anymore.

An unusual quiet and emptiness greeted us when Gregor and I got back to Mom's house. I roamed aimlessly from room to room with no sense of purpose. I knew I needed to get into task mode, but it was just too much to bear. Gregor had me sit down with him and we quietly watched TV until the TV started watching us. I was restless and didn't nod off for long.

I grabbed my laptop while Gregor slept, and began drafting the words that would be placed in the memorial service program. Mom was quite clear on what she wanted when it came to a funeral. She insisted on being cremated, she didn't want a church funeral, and she wanted nothing to do with being on display in an open casket. *"I don't want people staring at me"*, she would always say. Some tried to fight me on that, but I knew my mother's wishes and that's what I was going to concern myself with.

The next morning, I contacted Mrs. Ellis, from Ellis Funeral Home, who was already in receipt of Mom. I told her we wanted to proceed with a simple service in their facility on Saturday, three days away. Mrs. Ellis had no problem accommodating us and was a great help in guiding me on what needed to be done, who needed to be called, and in dealing with creating the program and obituary listing for the local newspapers.

The Ellis family was amazingly kind and professional with us and helped me get through the unforeseen madness that was soon to come. Tonya and the Grimes family were gems as well, as they thought of things that didn't even occur to me. They kept me steady and focused on Mom's wishes and how this would all be a tribute to her.

Gordon did arrive the day of the service. The funeral home was filled with Mom's friends and family members who gathered to pay their last respects. Tonya was so strong for me and spoke when I could not. My niece sang, the pastor from Shepard of the City spoke, and we passed out tiny plants that were part of a memorial wreath to all in attendance, in memory of Mom.

That's what took place on the surface...but would you like to know what *really* happened next?

To even begin to go into all the details of all the crap that happened between the moment my mother died and when Gregor and I got on that plane back to California would just take up too much space and energy. So here's the condensed version:

First: Linda got upset with me for not putting her name in the newspaper obituary. Mind you, I was on autopilot when I went into "task-mode" the night Mom died. I wrote only one long obituary for the memorial service program, which did include Linda. When I gave it to Mrs. Ellis, she asked what was I going to use for the newspaper? I asked if she could use the one I just gave her. She said she could but it was long it would end up costing me over two hundred dollars to post in the two local newspapers.

Damn, who knew? Mom had no insurance, had refinanced her house - leaving a mortgage behind, and no one was helping us financially with any of the arrangements. So, I asked Mrs. Ellis to help me trim it down for the papers. I couldn't think straight and I knew she was a pro at putting these things together. I deferred to Mrs. Ellis' expertise. She advised me to keep it simple by stating *when* Mom died and how she was survived by Gordon and me, as we were Mom's birth children. My head was spinning with too many things to tend to and Mrs. Ellis offered to help me eliminate this one additional task. No malice to offend my sister in this matter had been intended, but she took it the wrong way, dredging up old family shit that never had anything to do with me.

While Linda and I share the same father, we never shared the same household. Her mother never raised me, nor did Opal Jean raise her. I know my mother had maintained a close and loving relationship with Linda over the years, even before I was born, but we never shared the same household. I tried to get Linda to understand when her mother died the year prior to Mom's, I did not complain about not being in the newspaper obituary or even the church program. Nevertheless, Linda berated me for, *"ruining her credibility"* with her job!

It was just too much to believe and the last thing I needed to deal with. I had held my mother's hand and watched her die less than forty-eight hours ago and here is this woman, my sister, fussing at me about a newspaper omission?! Despite my apology and explanation, and the subsequent listing of her in the memorial service program, she remains, to this day, upset with me.

Second: The "good" reverend *(let's just leave his name out of this for now),* ripped us off for eighty dollars. It turns out the funeral home paid him prior to the service and I went and paid him in person the next day at his church, *and he said nothing!* I guess he thought it was a bloody tip… Really? All in the name of God, right?

Third: Gordon did not arrive until Saturday morning, just hours before the memorial service. His wife, Monica, was tipping back drinks of Jack Daniels and insisting that I allow her to smoke her funky cigarettes in my mother's house because, *"Opal once told me I could…"*. Are you kidding me? And *no*, she did not smoke in my mother's house.

Fourth: Cousin Mildred and her adult children came by to get their pick of Mom's stuff. Now, I had no problems with Mildred, even though she is bossy as all get-out. I had told her she could have the refrigerator, the VCR, and one of the TVs. But her daughter, who didn't send a card, nor come to the memorial service, was going through Mom's clothes and dishes looking for things to take *without first asking me if it was okay*. Even when I busted her for packing up my mother's china without asking, she proceeded to try and walk out of the house with the china! She claimed she did not know I wanted it, even though I had just mentioned it less than minutes previously. Common courtesy says to ask if you're not sure.

Fifth: Related to the obituary incident, a relative close to Linda called my mother's house that evening after the funeral and fussed out Gregor for "disrespecting" Linda during the memorial service at the funeral home. At the service Aunt Mable, Gordon, Gregor and I were seated in the front. I was told that Linda was sitting way in the back. I really didn't want her to feel bad by sitting away from us even though I knew she was still upset over the obituary issue.

Because Aunt Mable was a wreck and I wanted to stay with her, I asked Gregor to go ask Linda to please join us in the front row. According to Gregor, he quietly approached

Linda, and politely asked her to come sit up front with us. Gregor said Linda became upset with him approaching her like that and accused him of trying to embarrass her in front of everyone. She refused to join us and was now upset with Gregor as well. I really didn't consider him asking her to join us an act of disrespect.

This relative calling my mother's house and upsetting us, on the day we laid her to rest, was just too much for me. I just couldn't wrap my head around the anger and hurt being hurled at us. At the time I thought, *Damn... Linda is my older sister...my family, and we both should be bigger than this.* At that moment I concluded that the problems between us were centered on some deeper and seriously unresolved issues that I could not take on and try to resolve. I just lost *my* mother, for God's sake! Damn!

We couldn't book our flight back to Pasadena fast enough. Over the next several days, we donated most of Mom's furniture, clothing, and possessions no one wanted, to the Salvation Army. I met with the nursing home and Aunt Mable's church family to work out their continued care and support of Auntie. Her Seventh Day Adventist Church had been amazingly supportive and incredibly helpful throughout this whole ordeal. Their pastor promised the church would maintain daily vigils with Auntie and would check in with me weekly. In fact, they were prepared to fight me, as they thought I was going to take her back to California. I reassured them I knew her home was in Fort Wayne and her love was with her church. I am so extremely grateful for their love and support of my Auntie.

Tonya remained steady and strong for us and I was sad to leave her, but she too promised to keep an eye on Aunt Mable for me. Gregor and I caught an early 6:00 a.m. flight on Thursday, March 17th back to California. What a journey.

22

SEVEN YEARS LATER...THE LESSONS
LEARNED

During the 49 days of my Mother's illness, I maintained a daily journal that documented every moment and "truth" that took place, from my point of view. I wanted to note every feeling, the good and the not so good, which occurred during her illness until the day she died. In spite of all the arguing, disagreements, and head butting that took place with my mother, I can say this; my mother's faith in God never wavered. She never blamed God, never questioned Him, nor did she ever cry or feel sorry for herself. I had no idea how strong a woman my mother really was. How I wish I had her strength.

Out of all of this, I've learned several things that I now call my life lessons; things that have helped me get through the pain of losing my mother. These lessons have helped me disperse the anger I held against God (and everyone for that matter) for such a long time since Mom's death and my Auntie's subsequent passing.

Lesson 1: It's Okay to Feel What You Feel

When tragedy hits us human beings, we usually go through the typical five emotional stages of grief: denial, anger, bargaining, depression and acceptance – and not necessarily in any particular order. Whether you subscribe to these stages or not, at some point we go through one or all of these emotions.

Some of us feel we need to race through the anger stage in order to be "presentable" and "good souls" and to "move on" for the sake of everyone else. Bullshit! You feel what you feel. *Period.* Forget about appearances - that's just to make *other* people feel less uncomfortable about that tragedy you've just gone through.

Do you think Holocaust victims "got over" what they went through? What about those of us who suffered loss, injury, and were affected by the 9/11 tragedy? Should we stop feeling anger, hurt, and sadness over that? No. You feel what you feel and to deny that is to deny yourself.

I hate when well-meaning people say, *"It's all for the best"* or *"You're lucky to have had her as long as you did."* That crap just pisses me off. Of course, it's true that Mom's pain and suffering is gone and she was seventy-three years old when I lost her, but it's still *not okay!*

Maybe it's because the cancer was found so late and had ravished her body so quickly. I was angry with her for not having annual physicals. Perhaps the cancer would have been detected earlier and she could have survived. With it hitting her so severely, I didn't have time to prepare for what was in store for her. My mother was the most influential person in my life and she was gone 49 short days after being diagnosed. It broke my heart. I miss her and will always miss her…and *that* is what's okay.

Fortunately, I learned to channel that energy, and what Mom taught me about helping others, into helping make life better for other individuals. I work at promoting annual preventative screenings, physicals, self-exams, and access to affordable health care so any abnormalities can possibly be detected earlier.

So, to those "well-meaning" friends and family: don't *tell* me how to feel, just be there for us. Trust that we will work through it at our own pace, not yours.

Lesson 2: The Big Cancer Lie

My faith in the medical world has wavered since Mom's death and the subsequent death of sweet Auntie Mable in 2008 from cancer in her brain and breast. In my opinion, cancer is the most fucked up disease out there. It's an ugly parasite that hits for no rhyme or reason and devours those unfortunate enough to get it.

I'm annoyed with all the so-called walks/runs/fit/dance "For The Cure" events that have been draining our pockets for *years* and yet we still don't have a fucking cure! Why doesn't someone just tell the truth? There's more money in the disease itself, *not* in the cure. Pharmaceutical companies make millions with their cancer medications, treatments, and trials, and we all pay the price for it with our lives and the lives of our loved ones.

For me, the truth is that there *is* a cure for cancer out there. Unfortunately, there's no money in it for those pushing the medications. I once recall someone saying, *"If all the powerful leaders of the world were stricken with cancer, I bet a cure would be found."* I can only wonder.

Lesson 3: Take Care of Yourself...and be an Advocate

When life deals you a devastating challenge like this, you really need to learn how to take care of yourself while taking care of that loved one. I failed in that area and it turned me into a beast to be around.

I will never forget how kind the staff was at the Hospice House and Cancer Services. I went back to Cancer Services to return the items they gave me to use for Mom. As I left, an employee stopped me, looked me in the eyes, and told me to take care of myself. Now, of course, I thought it was the obligatory well wishes a stranger tells another stranger in passing, but this was different. She stopped me, held my hand and looked me in the eyes with a sincerity that touched my soul. *"No, really. You have to remember to take care of yourself."* I paused, squeezed her hand, and thanked her for caring.

She was right. I ate and shopped myself into a funk throughout the entire 49-day experience. That behavior did not help matters and it also hurt my health and sanity. Throughout my life I have tried to maintain a few, solid, "true" friends whom I could depend upon in times like these. I know I should have allowed them in sooner, but my pride and fear of not being in control prevented me from doing so. *Hmmm, sounds like someone I know!*

Do yourself a favor and find someone you trust to lean on. It may be a lifelong friend; but it could also be a complete stranger, like a pastor or a counselor. Whoever you choose, try to connect with them early on before your crisis turns you into a manic "beast". Once you start spinning out of control, it'll be difficult to think straight and even more difficult to get the support you really need.

Also, keep your health in check. As hard as it may be, we need to take a stand with loved ones, AND ourselves, to get annual physical exams and preventative health screenings. Early diagnosis is our friend when it comes to combating those sneaky illnesses that creep up without warning. Those of us who now have health coverage really have no excuse to not get checked. Go prepared with questions you may have regarding ANY problems you've been experiencing, no matter how small. Many times our elders, especially in the African-American community, do not *dare* question their physicians or ask questions when things don't make sense. This dangerous habit is getting passed on to our generation. We have to break this cycle of complacency and stop being content that what the doctor says is gospel! Ask questions; challenge their reasons for procedures that don't make sense to you. Be your own best advocate!

Lesson 4: Family is Family – Love Them Regardless
I harbor no ill will or bad feelings toward my sister, my brother, his wife or my cousins. I know I wasn't the easiest person to be around. Plus, they were dealing with the loss of Mom in their own way too. That's the other hateful thing

about death and loss - it's impossible to see what others are going through when you are blinded by your own grief. We are all unique, loving individuals who Mom loved deeply in her own special way. For better or worse, my family *is* my family and I love them regardless of what went down.

Mom understood Gordon better than I ever could. She knew it would be too hard for him to watch her go through what she went through. That day Gordon called the hospital and spoke with Mom, I saw a light in her that was genuine and loving toward her son. Days after they spoke, I made some snide remark about him and she told me that I should not be so hard on my brother. She explained that Gordon was more sensitive than he lets on. Mom recalled a time when he was nine and I was six: our dog jumped the fence, ran out into the street and got killed by a car. Mom said Gordon was more torn up about it than I was. Mom wanted me to understand that I was the stronger of the two of us when it came to matters of life and death.

At first I thought, "*Damn, he's no longer nine-years-old and he should be here with me!*" Still, the more Mom spoke of her son, the more I saw that she was okay with how he is. Hell, if Gordon not being there through all of this was fine with her, then who am I to be angry with him for not going through the drama with me? Mom understood the uniqueness of her children and loved us both the same.

Mom shared a special relationship with Linda, and she cherished the lovely and intelligent woman my sister had become. While I was not privy first-hand to all the issues between our father and her mother, it made no difference to Mom in how she related to her. Mom embraced Linda and told me stories where she helped her, spent time with her, and even assisted in getting her a prom dress when she was in high school.

I know our father's mental illness helped drive this wedge between my sister and I because of how he treated us so differently. My lack of knowledge of the happenings that transpired between her and Dad prior to my birth has not helped matters either. Perhaps, in time, we can be a family again. I certainly hope so.

Lesson 5: Tell Your Story

I began writing this story back in 2005 after what would have been my mother's 74th birthday. I stopped after the first sixty pages; my excuse being that "life" got in the way. Hubby and I produced a couple of short films, I was busy finding meaningful employment, etc., etc. The truth was that *I* kept getting in my own way when it came to finishing this story.

The more I shared with a select few about the book I had started about my mother, more interest piqued as to what it was about. Sadly, the painful truth of the story is what kept me from finishing it until now. The many mementos I have that remind me of Mom, (her orange *Bowlerette* tee shirt, her old cast-iron skillet, her worn recipe card for those amazing rolls), are things I cherish in the solitude of my home. However, this story, a story about the strongest woman I knew, was meant to be heard and shared outside the safety of my home. Not only that, but folks need to hear the honest feelings this daughter felt during those 49 days.

We owe it to ourselves to tell our stories when it comes to love, pain, loss, and suffering, no matter how difficult, no matter how long it takes. I am a storyteller, and this is a story about a woman named Opal Jean – through a daughter's eyes.

THE END

ABOUT THE AUTHOR

A native of Fort Wayne, Indiana, Natalie graduated from Bowling Green State University with a Bachelor's degree in Education and Music. She furthered her studies at New York City's Hunter College completing courses toward a Masters in Social Work.

For over 30 years Natalie has worked passionately offering aid to children and families for communities in Indiana, Ohio, New York City, and now Los Angeles. Always one to combine her love for social work and the arts, Ms. Manns engaged the youth she worked with by coaching and directing them in choirs, plays, and staged readings. An avid composer, songwriter and vocalist, she also flexed her own performance muscles touring nationwide in two Broadway musicals and singing in exclusive New York City jazz clubs including Sardi's, Tavern on the Green, and B Smith's.

Ms. Manns' first feature screenplay, *Truth* (co-written with Vernetta Cousins) was submitted into the 2002 Sundance

Feature Film Project competition where it reached the final round of competition. Although it did not win, it garnered interest by a production company who optioned *Truth* in 2003 to produce it into a feature film.

Natalie and her husband moved to California in 2004. Natalie quickly became educated in the art of digital video editing, and found a passion creating actor's performance reels. Seeing the need for creative, affordable demo reels, Natalie created *Yours By Design*, a demo reel editing service for actors. Through word of mouth and referrals, Natalie has created and edited over 200 demo reels and videos including America's Next Top Model, Nijah Harris, and the LA County Department of Public Health who published a Community Services reel on their website she helped create.

In 2007 Natalie and her husband created and co-founded MannsMade Productions, an independent film production company focused on fostering creativity and positive expression. Natalie made her film directorial debut in 2007 with MannsMade Production's first comedic short, *"Before and After"*, which she also wrote and received a "Best Comedy" nomination at the 2008 San Diego Black Film Festival. They went on to write and produce three additional short films that found successful runs in over 25 festivals.

MannsMade Productions won the 2010 DV Award for Outstanding Achievement in Digital Video Production for their drama *"Somebody's Gonna Pay"*. Their documentary, *"The Five Acres' Digital Storytelling Experience"*, a piece written and directed by Natalie about her work with the foster children, won Best Documentary Short at the 2014 Los Angeles Cinema Festival Of Hollywood.

Throughout all of her creative endeavors, Natalie enjoys spending her days working at a "regular job" assisting families and children. Currently employed with the Los Angeles County Department of Public Health, Ms. Manns works to reduce individual and community problems through creating and monitoring evidence-based programs designed to promote the health and well being of more than 10 million Los Angeles County residents.

Made in the USA
Lexington, KY
23 September 2015